A CASEBOOK ON
THE STAND

MORE WILDSIDE CLASSICS

Please see www.wildsidepress.com for a complete list!

A CASEBOOK ON THE STAND

Edited by
TONY MAGISTRALE

WILDSIDE PRESS

A CASEBOOK ON THE STAND

This edition published in 2006 by Wildside Press, LLC.
www.wildsidepress.com

Studies in Literary Criticism #38

A Casebook On

THE STAND

Tony Magistrale, Editor

R. REGINALD
The Borgo Press
San Bernardino, California

ABOUT THE CONTRIBUTORS

BERNADETTE BOSKY has long been an active contributor to scholarship on Stephen King. A Ph.D. candidate at Duke University, she has taught for many years at colleges around the Durham, North Carolina area.

ED CASEBEER is a Professor of English at Indiana University where he teaches courses in popular culture and American studies. For several years he has been writing about the role of communities in Stephen King's novels.

LEONARD CASSUTO is an Assistant Professor of English at Fordham University where he is presently at work on a book-length project analyzing the role of the grotesque in nineteenth-century American literature.

STEVEN E. KAGLE is a Professor of English at Illinois State University. He was an editor of the journal *Exploration*, a publication that specialized in travel and exploration literature.

DOUGLAS KEESEY is the editor of two forthcoming collections of essays—on *It* and *Pet Sematary*—which will join this present volume as critical casebooks in the Starmont House library on Stephen King. Prof. Keesey teaches in the English department at Cal Poly State University.

BRIAN KENT is an Instructor of English at the University of Vermont, and a free-lance writer and editor. He teaches a course in popular literature entitled "The American Best-Seller," that always includes at least one representative work by Stephen King.

TONY MAGISTRALE has written and/or edited several books on Stephen King and the American Gothic. He is an Associate Professor of English at the University of Vermont where he teaches a course entitled "The Films and Novels of Stephen King."

MICHAEL A. MORRISON is a Professor of Physics at Oklahoma University. In addition to contemplating the mysteries of the universe, he also teaches courses in science-fiction, and has published extensively on Stephen King and other writers in the genre of the fantastic. He edits *Necrofile: A Review of Horror Fiction.*

LEONARD MUSTAZZA is an Associate Professor of English at Penn State University. He is the author of books and articles on Stephen King, Kurt Vonnegut, and John Milton.

MARY PHARR is an accomplished scholar on film and in studies in the fantastic, and several of her essays on Stephen King have appeared in collections of criticism on his work. She teaches in the English department at Florida Southern College.

For my friends at Stonehedge:
Dawn, Phil, Mia, Katie, Judy, Leslie, and Finkle

TABLE OF CONTENTS

INTRODUCTION

Over the years, much has been written about the amount of writing published by Stephen King. For some, the sheer quantity is evidence enough that he will never be a master craftsman of literate prose; for others, the size of his books is just another "American" aspect of King: he writes big narratives that grapple with fundamental philosophical issues. For those truly interested in King's language output, a visit to the University of Maine, Orono library is a definite necessity. In the room devoted to Stephen King's collected manuscripts, it is possible not only to view the successive typescript drafts of novels (filling a dozen cardboard boxes) which have become icons of contemporary popular culture, but to marvel at the amount of fiction and political/literary commentary that has remained—and to my understanding, will continue to remain—unpublished. Several complete early novels are presently housed in this archive, as is much of the writing he produced for the UMO college newspaper as an undergraduate. But what is perhaps most intriguing for the King specialist are the unpublished, heavily edited drafts of King's most important novels and short fiction. Reviewing the edited manuscripts of any famous artist is an exhilarating undertaking: well-known passages, phrasing, and scenes are suddenly placed in a startling context when juxtaposed with unfamiliar language that, for better or worse, has been discarded by the author from the published version. This is especially true when perusing the manuscripts of Stephen King, as whole sections of The Shining and Christine (the two examples I recall most vividly) were cut from the final drafts appeared like someone's neglected children in need of attention.

The Stand was rescued from a similar fate when, in 1990, King released the "complete and uncut" edition of the novel. The book, however, is not merely the restored text as it was originally composed in 1978. As Mary Pharr and Douglas Kessey point out in their respective essays which begin this collection, King has continued to edit and revise the novel: moving the dates of the apocalypse forward, changing names of politicians and popular performers, and generally establishing a more contemporary backdrop for the events which unfold. Aside from these rather cosmetic alterations, the "restored" edition of The Stand strikes this reader as an infinitely better book than was originally released in 1978. Not only is this larger volume a richer text in terms of the additional material supplied about characters and the consequences of the disaster itself, the 1990 edition also appears more "complete"—that is, there is a greater degree of symmetry to this version that is immediately apparent when compared to the original publication.

To a greater or lesser degree, each of the contributors to this volume of essays addresses the differences between these two versions of The Stand. In addition, Mary Pharr's "Surviving the Plague in Stephen King's The Stand" and Doug Keesey's "Stephen King's Stand on Politics" discuss the roles politics and technology play both in creating the superflu disaster and in the aftermath as the survivors seek to reestablish new social bonds. Brian Kent's piece, "Stephen King and His Readers: A Dirty, Compelling Romance," considers both the demographics and personalities represented in Stephen King's massive audience, acknowledging the writer's attraction to, and utilization of, high and low culture and his consequent appeal to a wide readership. Leonard Cassuto's contribution, "The Power of Blackness in The Stand," establishes the intertextual relationships between King's novel, nineteenth-century American literature, and the Puritan influence on both. Leonard Mustazza's "Repaying Service with Pain: The Role of God in The Stand" discusses King's own Methodist upbringing in light of the divine manifestation found in The Stand. My own contribution to this volume, "Free Will and Sexual Choice in The Stand," highlights the role of sexuality as a barometer for measuring individual morality in the novel. Bernadette Bosky is also interested in the issue of personal choice in her essay, "Choice, Sacrifice, Destiny, and Nature in The Stand," although she is less concerned with the secular implications of "good decision-making" than with its impact upon the novel's cosmic struggle between good and evil. Michael

Morrison's "Dark Streets and Bright Dreams: Rationalism, Technology, and 'Impossible Knowledge,'" argues that the novel gradually extols interpersonal telepathy-dreams, visions, and other evidence of mystical phenomena—as superior to technology for sustaining human communication and survival. Ed Casebeer's "Dialogue within the Archetypal Community of The Stand" is a study in the narratology of the text; Prof. Casebeer is interested in analyzing the narrative perspective employed in relaying events to the reader. Lastly, Stephen Kagle's "Beyond Armageddon" examines The Stand and seeks to place it in the tradition of speculative fiction. He reads King's novel from the perspective of a science fiction theorist rather than a King specialist.

A Casebook on The Stand was one of the final projects Ted Dikty, long-time editor at Starmont House and a man to whom Stephen King scholarship is immeasurably indebted, commissioned for publication. After the release of The Shining Reader (1991), the first volume he envisioned in a series of critical anthologies each devoted to a single King text, Ted seemed anxious to push the other projected volumes forward. Although always an astute businessman, Ted's anxiousness on this occasion had less to do with capitalizing upon Stephen King's enormous popularity than with his belief that these books might indeed advance King criticism to an enhanced level of discourse. Ted hoped these casebooks might eventually become core, "self-contained" resources for students, scholars, and fans seeking the most complete range of critical interpretations on King's fiction. The essays in this volume were assembled with Ted's vision in mind; my only regret is that he will never get the opportunity to read them himself and to delight in the accomplishment for which he is more than partly responsible.

Tony Magistrale
University of Vermont
Burlington, Vermont
January 1992

xii

CHAPTER ONE

"Almost Better": Surviving the Plague in Stephen King's The Stand

Mary Pharr

On a first reading, Stephen King's The Stand seems to be a novel about three related but distinct events: the pandemic plague that decimates most of the Earth's population, the hazardous trek of the plague's survivors to opposing camps whose leaders first appear in dreams, and the apocalyptic struggle engaged in by these camps. Epic in theme and structure, The Stand pulls its readers along on the journey from a world of petty misery and moral ambivalence to a new world of great danger and greater possibility. By its very title, the book focuses on the end of this journey, when the forces of a demon are openly arrayed against those men and women aligned with God, when the balance between universal good and evil is threatened by a chaos far older than any plague. In this part of his novel, King takes his reader across the boundary between mortal catastrophe and eternal peril. And when the hand of God and the small sacrifice of flesh together drive back the devil and maintain the balance in things, readers are left with the kind of wary but genuine hope that the plague-bound portion of the story seems unable to provide. It's easy to cling to this hope and let the first third of the story slip away as a kind of very unpleasant means to a delayed but worthy end.

King himself has actually fostered this view by referring more than once to the Alexandrian compulsion he felt as he used plague to decimate his novel's world. According to the author, the plague serves as a means of cutting the "Gordian knot," of "envisioning an entire entrenched societal process destroyed at a stroke" (Danse Macabre, 373; cf. Bare Bones, 30). With the simple, horrifying expedient of a disease that rapidly fells 99.4% of Earth's population, King cuts through all the ordinary concerns of mundane

American society, leaving a country—and, by inference, a planet—newly stripped of all economic, political, and bureaucratic burdens. Thus, he has one character bitterly inform another that by creating the plague, the "people in authority" have "solved the depressed economy, pollution, the oil shortage and the cold war, all at a stroke" (252). That stroke becomes the author's emblem.

And there is something else the author admits to as well. In Danse Macabre, King writes of the "crazy, joyful feeling" he experienced while writing The Stand (371-2). He goes on to identify this feeling as a natural reaction, a means of escaping both the national problems of the '70's and his personal frustrations in the first years of his fame. By swinging the Alexandrian sword, King found a way to relieve his own tensions, to lessen that sense that most men feel even in the good times that they are somehow trapped by forces that no individual can control. In general, well-balanced adults do not admit to their Alexandrian desires, but at least a part of this work's appeal is its creator's intuitive understanding of how universal those desires are—if only in dreams.

Nonetheless, the ultimate function of the plague within this novel is more than magic bullet, more even than a release valve, certainly more than a grim contrivance to carry the plot to an epic arena. Known as Captain Trips during its few weeks of vicious life, the plague of superflu initially shapes the conflict between good and evil in this book and then presages the ambiguous answer King here provides regarding the role of man within that struggle. A byproduct of both institutionalism and technology, Captain Trips slams through the cant of twentieth-century civilization to reveal just how weak the supports that prop up most social structures are and just how much most people need the illusion of those supports. Surviving the superflu is not just a matter of genetic luck (though enormous luck is needed), nor is it any kind of moral judgment (though a sense of inevitability prevails throughout King's epic). The fact is that the flu survivors at the center of this tale all share a disaffection with social norms or mores, a disaffection that has somehow isolated them from the rigidly organized structures

2

from whence the Captain springs. As the structures reappear, survivors lose their isolation and, too often, their lives as well; yet the work also acknowledges the inevitability, even desirability, of such structures in the human experience. King begins and ends his book with references to a circle opening (xiv) and closing (1150), and the circular nature of existence is his final subject. The plague is his means of defining that circle. What is startling and yet credible about the plague itself is that everyone is amazed at its occurrence. Mulling over the string of unlucky events and simple blunders that led to the plague's wide dissemination, one high-ranking officer calls the situation "a chain of coincidence on the order of winning the Irish Sweepstakes" (32). A little later, when Stu Redman, the novel's central male protagonist, demands to know who was responsible for this virulent outbreak of disease, the tough-minded colonel he talks to has a curiously offhand response: the contaminated soldier who initially spread the disease by running from his post could be held accountable, but "under the circumstances, you or I might have run, too" (110). Moreover, it was "a technical slipup" that allowed the frightened guard to escape the base (110), the sort of error that is inevitable in the course of time. It's quite clear from what the men in charge think and say that while they accept the general liability of everyone involved in the incident, they find no individual responsibility assignable at all. Captain Trips seems to have come on the backs of many men—and at the hands of nobody at all.

In effect, then, the accident that creates the superflu one California night is simply part of a historical configuration; unfortunately, it comes at a time when the world—two hundred years into the Industrial Revolution—can ill afford such a configuration. Civilizations have always risen and fallen by the human need to gather into groups that grow too large to sustain their initial vision, with original values giving way to structure and its children: incompetence and corruption. Ancient civilizations, like the empires of Egypt, Greece, and Rome, disintegrated into detritus over a period of centuries; but modern science squeezes the process of detrition into a matter of weeks, days, even hours.

3

Even more frightening is the propensity of technology to leap away from its creator, to move out of human control long before mankind has carefully considered the ethical issues of new scientific application. What seems to worry Stephen King most about this propensity is its connection to the worst aspects of socialization. Thus, as Tony Magistrale has noted, King's "novels and tales often link governmental bureaucracies and science in an unholy tryst: both tinker blindly and immorally with aspects of nature they neither respect nor comprehend" (51). Many of the denizens of our aptly named Age of Anxiety feel a similar concern, but King carries that concern to an extreme (resulting, on occasion, in the kind of heavy-handed paranoia that guides The Golden Years, King's 1991 TV series full of caricatures rather than characters: e.g. a mad scientist who looks and acts like Bozo and a sleazy government agent who off-handedly massacres the occupants of a commune for the crime of clinging to a 1960's sensibility). In The Stand, however, particularly in its unexpurgated form, the intensity of the author's attitude toward errant technology and social disintegration is both believable and justified. Douglas Winter has pointed out that in this novel King forces us to admit that "Our position as a society is a precarious one—and principally because of our misguided belief in the divinity of civilization and technology" (58). Thus, the roots of evil within this epic lie as much—or more—in human weakness as in any demonic influence.

For the truth is, as Glen Bateman, the novel's resident philosopher, wryly notes, "we are hooked" on technology (347). Millions of people have lived and millions more died during this century due to our obsession with the power and the glamour of technology. Captain Trips itself is a left-handed salute to modern ingenuity, far more virulent in its protean horror than the bubonic and pneumonic plagues it displaces in the history of pandemics. There is nothing natural about this plague: it is not a cancer but an invention, an invention apparently perceived as a defensive weapon despite the 99+ kill factor built into its technology. In that respect, this product of what the government all too appropriately calls Project Blue is just like all the nuclear weapons, chemical agents, and germ warfare schemes that exist in actuality. Interest in such schemes is, on some level, almost always theoretical. The danger of such theory can be seen in a sign found on a corpse slumped over in a corner of the research facility that produced the superflu: "NOW YOU KNOW IT WORKS. ANY QUESTIONS?" (178).

Unfortunately, as Stu Redman slowly realizes, it's too late to ask questions. The systematic deaths within Project Blue are just the first of billions of fatalities. When the American government realizes that it has really lost control of the superflu, it disseminates the disease around the globe as quickly as it can, using the all too appropriate code, "Rome falls" (175). The military commander who orders this dispersal of death tells his subordinate that "no one will ever know," that "our opposite numbers may suspect, but there won't be time enough" (175). The irony of this nebulous rationalization is that it is justified. If anyone in the world is to survive, almost everyone must die. The plague cannot be stopped by quarantines; indeed, it's no more than marginally slowed by the most extreme measures. A last-minute nuclear attack by a maddened enemy of the U.S. would merely delay the inevitable epidemic while almost certainly killing the few men and women immune to the flu. Technology guided by the imperfect mind of man has caught him in a bind from which he cannot emerge unscathed. The commander who orders the global infusion of plague shoots himself soon after. Unfortunately, the sound of the shot is too soft to be heard amid the wails of a dying civilization.

Soon thereafter, anarchy descends. Captain Trips moves so quickly that the President of the United States barely has time to say, "There is no truth—no truth—to the rumor that this strain of flu is fatal" (229) before he and most of his listeners are dead. Many die like singer Larry Underwood's mother, a decent older woman who ends her life "lying on a cot in the hallway of [New York's] Mercy Hospital" trapped amid "the stench of urine and feces, the hell's babble of the delirious, the choking, the insane, the screams of the bereaved" (236). But as in the California laboratory, not all fatalities are, strictly

5

speaking, caused by superflu. Military forces at both the state and the federal level rip through America using their high-tech equipment to bury diseased bodies, destroy dissident communications, and murder angry malcontents—not an easy task since virtually everyone everywhere is distinctly malcontented. As the soldiers themselves sicken, panic, and die, riots and insurrection replace oppression. Here a female student is "cut in half by gunfire" (224), there a graying sergeant is executed "like a disintegrating puppet" (227), and even a heartland city like Des Moines falls to a riot that ends having "gutted most of the downtown area" (228). In truth, the Captain really is considerably more robust than the Chief Executive, and it has no difficulty at all knocking down the structures of an entire culture.

Sadly and inescapably, some of those who are immune to the virus are not immune to its effects. One of the truest and most touching chapters in the Complete Edition of The Stand is the one that details what the author calls the "second epidemic" (350), the wave of deaths attributable to the absence of civilization as the pandemic winds down. The casualties here fall not to the flu or the government or even chaos but to their own inability to survive in a world that has suddenly lost all of its social framework and much of its technology. For as authority and organization dissolve, routine elements of security and comfort (e.g. all electrical utilities) simply cease to function. Both metaphorically and literally, the lights go out all over the world.

For those who are genetically excused from catching the plague, there is a choice: give up or go on. Giving up means extinction through the second epidemic; going on means responding to the larger context of whatever lies beyond apocalypse, taking a stand one way or another in the universal struggle between the sacred and the profane. Such a response is fundamental to King's Romantic mentality, to his fascination with the need to make choices, to affect life rather than to drift with it. Moreover, like Rousseau, Goethe, and Wordsworth, the great initiators of the Romantic tradition, King admires those who refuse to submit to social restrictions. Thus, the main characters in The Stand, all survivors of the superflu and its initial aftershock, are also all to a greater or lesser degree detached from bourgeois society. Whether good, evil, or in a state of moral flux, these solitary figures have precisely the temperament required to live for at least a while without institutions and technology.

The isolation of the central characters in this novel cuts to the core of the human experience as King perceives it. Clive Barker has described King's vision as "Not the vision of the *better* economy, the *better* combustion engine, the *better* Eden," but a vision where survival is dependent on "our intimacy with our dark and dreaming selves" (69). Here King parts company with the High Romantics and shows instead his Gothic side, his Dark Romantic ability to see the skull beneath the skin—an ability he imparts to both the heroes and villains of The Stand. By circumstances of birth, by a decision of the will, or by the actions of others, these central figures have sensed too much of the grit beneath the glitter of society to abide its constraints easily. Once those constraints are broken, however, King's disaffected protagonists and alienated antagonists are free to save or destroy what is left of the world. Abruptly, they turn from dreamers into doers by the shattering of the technological and cultural *zeitgeist* that had earlier separated them from society. In the context of these liberated survivors, it is quite appropriate that the plague proper ends on July 4. It is even more appropriate that these men and women learn of the choice they must now make through the dim medium of dreams, visions that inspire them to journey through darkness toward destiny.

The focal points of these dreams are Mother Abagail Freemantle and Randall Flagg, the anointed representatives of God and the Devil, the old woman and the dark man who must marshall the survivors of the plague into forces of good and evil—both sides, ironically, uncertain of their purpose, both sides bound uneasily to the mysteries of the Lords of Hosts and Demons. Like the other central figures in this book, Mother Abagail and the Walkin Dude are themselves isolated from the mainstream of American society, she by reason of her race, age, and sex; and he by his very nature, his essential inability to do ought but destroy.

7

The old lady has the shine, the prophetic "shining lamp of God" as she calls it (513), and she saw apocalypse two years before it happened. Yet as with the prophets of all religions, Mother Abagail will be heard only in profound crisis. Indeed, she herself would prefer not to hear the voice that speaks to her: "Those dreams they scared me. I even tried to pretend they was just dreams, foolish old woman runnin from God the way Jonah did" (513). Like Jonah, Mother Abagail has the faint hint of absurdity about her as she turns from an anonymous crone to the voice of God. Her initial trip through darkness comes as she walks home from a neighbor's house, all the while protecting a few chickens from a hoard of attacking weasels. But the weasels belong to the dark man, and the chickens are meant to feed the first who will oppose him; so after thinking of the Lord, the prophet protects her charges. Protecting humanity, however, will not be such a short and triumphant journey.

As for the this prophet's nemesis, Randall Flagg is a demon—but not the Demon. If he is far more eager than Mother Abagail to lead mankind into the apocalypse, he is also far more obtuse than the old woman about just who he is and what he serves. Certainly, Flagg is evil incarnate, but he is also folly incarnate, something that appears to Stu Redman in a dream as a creature with "No soul, but a sense of humor" (349). In truth, Flagg is a petty monster, his goal nothing more than dictatorship and his power merely that of limited magic, hypnotic skill, and mechanical devices. Nonetheless, he is immensely dangerous. At his core there is, as Tony Magistrale has observed, "the same impulses toward self-destruction and betrayal that characterize King's portrait of modern technology" (43-4). In fact, Glen Bateman calls Flagg "just the last magician of rational thought, gathering the tools of technology against us" (742).

The irony here is the irony of the accident at Project Blue. Like germ warfare, the dark man's *raison d'etre* is destruction. In former times he was the shadowy figure behind a variety of "riots, overturned cars, student strike votes, and violent demonstrations" (183-4). In the year of the plague, however, he is more than just the irritant behind angry radicals: he is the spirit and mechanism—social and technical—that created the superflu out walking around even after the flu itself has dissipated. He will use the same organization and science that destroyed most of the world first to subjugate and then annihilate what's left. In Flagg, Captain Trips journeys on.

Thus, the plague mentality is carried unseen into the epic arena, where it becomes a crucial part of the spiritual weaponry wielded by both sides. In his preface to the unexpurgated Stand, King calls his epic a "long tale of dark Christianity" (xii), and he uses the plague as the device on which his theology turns. Philip Ziegler, in his seminal work on the bubonic and pneumonic plagues in Europe, has noted the shift from complacent faith to fanatic devotion among the survivors of the worst pandemic in history:

> The terrors of the Black Death drove man to
> seek a more intense, a more personal relationship
> with the God who thus scourged him, it led him out
> of the formal paths of establishment religion and, by
> only a short remove, tumbled him into the darkest pit
> of Satanism. The Europeans of the 1350s and 1360s
> were no more saints or devils than their ancestors but
> such emotional disturbance had been generated that
> they were often within a step of believing themselves
> one or the other. They had been tested to the utter-
> most and even a touch was henceforth enough to tip
> them from their precarious balance. (277)

Like their predecessors in enduring the unendurable, King's sur-vivors need both the numinous and the spectral, the undying assurance that there is more to the universe than that which man has devised. The dreams that play so critical a role in this book are explicitly extrasen-sory in form and theological in substance; they are an invitation to connect with someone or something that seems to be both fundamen-tally superior and extraordinarily powerful. In time, the offer proves if not illusory then at least circular—taking its recipients back to them-

9

selves and the world back to its former ways. But for a while, at least, and for those who were never wholly comfortable with the old system, the invitation to either sainthood or deviltry is an unexpected offer that is simply irresistible.

Thus, from the state of Texas comes Stu Redman, once "the quietest man in Arnette" (4), once a widower with no children and a meaningless job, now a critical member of Mother Abagail's—that is, God's team. Stu is too decent to consider the plague his once-in-a-lifetime opportunity to escape the trivial role society has assigned him; nonetheless, Captain Trips does set him free. He leaves a life of simple loneliness, a dull dependence on the technology of the calculator factory that employs him, and an aching certainty that he will remain nothing more than "another good old boy in a dying Texas town" (5). He becomes the man who knows more than any other survivor about the origin of the plague, then the strong arm of justice among other survivors, and, finally, the new Adam chosen to replenish the Earth with his beautiful new Eve.

That Eve is Frannie Goldsmith, the girl from Ongunquit, Maine, who has more than Stu has before the plague—more hope and more trauma. Tall, intelligent, and good-looking, Frannie is the very model of a romantic heroine; she is also pregnant by a boy she doesn't love. Like many bright young women in 1990, Frannie counted on technology to keep her safe (an ironic faith in the context of the situation developing in Project Blue just across the continent). And as in California, something went askew in Maine, and the pill hadn't worked, maybe because somebody at the Ovril factory was "asleep at the switch" (14), maybe because she herself had forgotten a pill and "then had forgotten she'd forgotten" (14). It never occurs to the eminently sensible and emphatically unspiritual Frannie that maybe Heaven wants her pregnant. All she sees is a selfish boyfriend she doesn't love, a cold mother who doesn't love her, and a caring, ineffectual father. For Frannie, suddenly, "a break with Ongunquit [is] necessary," a break with the streets where she can "feel people, not looking at her, but *getting ready* to look at her" (164). The superflu solves that problem, and, though it costs Frannie the agonizing loss of both her parents, it makes her baby not a cause for pity or derision but a source of hope to the other survivors. Like Stu, like so many others in this book, the meaning of Frannie's life is determined by the pandemic. Yet none of it is easy. Both Douglas Winter and Tony Magistrale have noted King's tendency to drive his characters through darkness on their way to definition (cf. Winter's reference to "night journeys" [2] and Magistrale's comments on tunnel imagery [90]). Indeed, everyone in The Stand journeys across America toward either Abagail's camp at Boulder, Colorado, or Flagg's post in Las Vegas; but the real epic odyssey begins much earlier for each of the survivors. In fact, for some of the survivors, the option to follow the well-worn paths of the old society never even existed. Nick Andros is, perhaps, the wisest of Mother Abagail's people; he is also a twenty-one year old deaf mute who has always been outside society. Yet he dies explicitly trying to save the lives of the reforming society of the Free Zone. Tom Cullen is surely the most innocent of men before and after the plague: a retarded adult, he is as well "God's Tom" (819), forever held apart from the rest of mankind not so much by his retardation as his inability to sin. Together, Nick and Tom reflect one of this novel's epic mysteries: not just that out of evil can come good, nor simply that disabilities often hide strengths; but that everyone and everything has its role, that if chaos suggests that nothing is certain, it also proves that everything matters. Nick and Tom are ignored and abused in the brightly lit, highly regulated world of Project Blue, but Nick's death and Tom's life matter enormously in the dark aftermath of Captain Trips.

The pattern continues, until virtually all of the novel's important characters reveal themselves to have been out of step with the *ancien regime*, yet in step now with the emerging struggle. There is Dayna Jurgens, a Free-Zone spy who is both beautiful and brave—and lesbian. There is the Judge, another Boulder spy whose intelligence and courage are evident to all, but whose advanced age would hold him to a marginal role in any pre-plague society. Even Glen Bateman, the sixty-year old sociologist with the wrong degree and rank (M.F.A. and assistant professor) for his job and age, says his former colleagues thought he "was a lunatic," (340), an assessment that obviously isolated him in the past but that now allows him to accept the superflu with more tranquility than most of the other survivors can manage.

On Flagg's side, the disaffected condition of the survivors is even more obvious. People like Julie Lawry, a foolish young tramp with no sense of morality but a natural affinity for the material rewards Flagg offers, and Barry Dorgan, a former policeman who prefers order to ethics, go to Las Vegas because it promises them power and position. They never get either, of course. Flagg's promises are as false as the dead government's promise of a flu vaccine. In fact, the dark man has a habit of dispatching any of his servants who prove unmanageable, most vividly, perhaps, the absolute psycho known as The Kid, a killer so independent and deranged as to be uncontrollable and, therefore, useless to the densely structured society Flagg creates in Nevada.

Most of the novel's major characters make their choice of Boulder or Las Vegas almost by instinct, but some of the survivors walk away from their pre-plague selves after conscious deliberation. Nadine Cross, for example, is a just a vaguely pitiful cliché before the flu—a striking old-maid English teacher with secret desires her students cannot imagine. Until the time of Captain Trips, she lives publicly for others, and people after the plague invariably expect the teacher to continue on this dull but righteous path. But Nadine has always secretly believed that she is special, destined for some overwhelming passion. All her life she has refused to integrate her sexual self and her ethical awareness. Now she loses the latter completely as she consciously decides to "choose whatever dark adventure" is left for her (775). Inexorably and stealthily, she drifts into Flagg's camp for the most unsavory of reasons: to be the bride of a demon. She gets her wish, though it proves to be as illusory as Flagg's other offers; and she dies not a virgin but a dupe of her own determination to separate her public and her private self.

Conversely, Larry Underwood learns to bring his behavior in line with his soul. Formerly a rock singer, Larry has always been a user, a man haunted by his mother's assessment that he has a "hard streak" in him, something harsh in his character that he has repeatedly wielded "as a bludgeon to beat his way out of traps he had dug for himself" (50). Larry doesn't dig the trap that Project Blue springs, however, and for the first time in his life he has a chance to use his hardness to pull others out of a pit. Or he could just live for himself, as he has lived in the past. The choice is a very private, very difficult one for this man who lacks Stu Redman's natural heroism, Glen Bateman's long-term philosophy, and Nick Andros' intuitive wisdom. Larry's journey through darkness toward self-awareness takes him literally through black tunnels and blacker temptations (with Nadine Cross as the focus of the latter), and all he really has to guide him is the toughness that he once despised in himself—that and a fundamental sense that a man can be both hard and decent if he chooses to be both. Larry makes his choice, and at The Stand in Las Vegas, this unlikely saviour dies fearing no evil and, finally, with no need to fear himself.

Nadine moves in one direction, Larry another; but both move away from the past. They become, in effect, pioneers of apocalypse, creating the future by their actions. Harold Lauder, on the other hand, is trapped not so much by Flagg as by his own past and his refusal to let that past go. Just a teenager when the plague takes his family, Harold is somehow the most complex character in this book: a boy with more potential than even Nick Andros, but a boy who knowingly allows himself to be seduced by the Walkin Dude's wiles (again in the form of Nadine Cross). In the *ancien regime*, Harold is the quintessential outsider: the boy both peers and adults instinctively loathe, the smart kid who's also a smart aleck, the fat kid who's too afraid to play sports, the slovenly kid who's never had a date. Even his parents find Harold distasteful, a fluky contrast to his popular sister, Amy, Frannie's best friend and the perfect American miss. Secure, apparently, in the normalcy of her budding sexuality, Amy is preparing for her wedding when Captain Trips comes by—and the wedding gown is never worn.

13

As for her brother, his incipient sexuality should be ready to flourish as well, but what stops Harold is not the plague but his own inability to acknowledge the physical and emotional equality of other people. Feeling himself snubbed, he responds with childish scorn toward his family and all the world. After the superflu, however, Harold knows as surely as Larry that he has a choice. Unfortunately, that choice turns on the sexual fixation he develops in regard to Frannie, who disliked him before the epidemic and who still finds him annoying. Nothing in Harold can match Stu Redman's quiet strength in crisis, the kind of strength that draws Frannie to Stu and completely away from Harold. Inevitably, the boy nurses his hatred for the ones who have what he cannot get.

Yet as the weeks go by and Harold's body toughens and his mind is challenged by the basic work of survival, the people of Boulder—the ones who have no reason to prejudge him—actually come to like this boy. Some even start to call him "Hawk" (796), a sign of the strength that they see coming out of this emerging man. Even as people are sensing what might be in Harold, however, he continues secretly nursing his private griefs against the world. The epitome of quick intelligence, he is also the epitome of childish inflexibility. He elects to embrace pride and hate, the very qualities the plague survivors are trying to eradicate; for as he writes in his journal, to give away such sins "is to say you will change for the good of the world;" to embrace them "is to say that the world must change for the good of you" (683). A victim of the same cold logic and puerile arrogance that created Project Blue, Harold thinks he can do anything without regard to consequences. He doesn't even really believe that the dark man is demonic—just "some sort of psychic" (732), full of power but accessible to Harold's genius. In the long run, Flagg uses and discards this boy. Only then, as he lies dying alone on a desolate cliff, does Harold grow up and write, "The dark man is as real as the superflu itself, as real as the atomic bombs that still sit somewhere in their leadlined closets" (977). Once he has accepted this hard reality, Harold finally understands that he "could have been something in Boulder" (978), could

have created rather than destroyed. In this realization, he dies—but as
the Hawk rather than as Harold, not so much in despair as in the full
awareness of his own responsibility and role. He shoots himself as a
conscious act of expiation; and in so doing, Harold Lauder finally recovers from the plague.

The world he leaves behind is, however, a different matter, as sus-
ceptible as it ever was to the forces that created Captain Trips. It
shouldn't really be that way. The survivors make choices, and the Free
Zone forms in direct opposition to Las Vegas; but the human propensity to institutionalism and technology remains—even in the formerly
disaffected, even in the ones who should have learned from their own
experience. Like the Biblical flood, the pandemic kills nearly everyone, yet it does not quite manage to eradicate the basic threat inherent in technology: that man will use it to exterminate all life on this
planet. When Flagg rapidly reassembles the despotic social structures
needed to deliver nuclear weapons (as Harold had obliquely prophesied), the threat returns—only to be squelched by God and His dis-
organized, ill-equipped band of the elect. The only offering the Lord
God seems to require is the death of most of the story's central figures:
among them Abagail, Nick, Larry, Glen, the Judge, Dayna, and, of
course, Harold. Ironically, the thousands who escaped the flu only to
be enticed by Flagg's tricks also die in the apocalyptic fire that metaphorically becomes the last fever in this outbreak of the plague. Afterwards, the world and its remaining inhabitants should truly be different, wiser—but that's not quite the way things work out.

The explanation may be found, perhaps, in the epidemiology of
the superflu. It is always on the move, snaking its way quite rapidly
around the defenses the body puts up, yet always returning to the attack until, finally, it kills its host. It does much of what AIDS does but
a thousand times faster. Moreover, as Joseph Reino has observed, the
shape-shifting nature of the flu is a direct reflection of Flagg himself,
who randomly changes his name—even his physical form—as a
manifestation of his demonic nature (57-8). As with the plague,
Flagg's manifestations continually confuse what few human defenses

there are against the demonic. In essence, some of those who fall to Captain Trips are "almost better" (1137) just before they die; so, too, is the world after The Stand against the dark man. One truly virulent version of a universal plague has been wiped out, but the source remains, merely shifting to another form.

At first, it looks as though the techno-social virus that Flagg represents is gone from the Free Zone, where Harold sees people as somehow "not the same as they had been" (682). Held by their vision of Mother Abagail and what—who—she represents, people don't need ceremonies in Boulder, they don't fight much, and they don't question those "profound theological implications of the dreams and of the plague itself" (682). Harold also understands that the Las Vegas society is a "single wild cell taken from the dying corpus of the old body politic, a lone representative of the carcinoma that had been eating the old society alive" (682). Harold chooses the malignancy, but one of the ironies of his choice is that he does not see that Boulder itself—so new and healthy on the surface—still carries the disease that destroyed almost everything within itself.

Glen has always understood this. Long before Boulder, Glen had prophesied that mankind's love of socialization and technology would drive survivors of the flu into little communities jealously guarding their power plants. Reorganization is rational, and as Glen adds much later, "At the end of all rationalism, the mass grave" (741). Like the others who are close to Mother Abagail, even the old sociologist comes to hope that a different mentality is being formed, but the citizens of both Las Vegas and Boulder, the ones not directly touched by a close encounter with either a demon or a saint, yet retain their rationalistic tendencies—and, eventually, those tendencies erupt.

It happens as the Free Zone expands, as it turns from a tiny theocracy into a functioning city-state. Mother Abagail wanders off to expiate her own sins, and as she returns in extremis, Harold and Nadine manage to kill Nick—just before the power is about to be switched back on in Boulder. When Stu tries to tell a vengeful and frightened meeting of the masses what has happened, he feels "disquieted and bewildered, as if the Free Zone had changed radically over the last forty-eight hours and he didn't know what it was anymore" (906). Stu's intuition is (like almost all the intuitive knowledge in this novel) accurate. For after God and history have been at least momentarily appeased by the many casualties lost in The Stand against evil, those who are left remain steadily at work recreating the world that created Captain Trips.

Within a year of the accident that released the superflu, people come streaming into Boulder by the thousands, and with them comes bureaucracy, even a Census Bureau working hard to count heads. With the old crisis committee dissolved by death, a new, secular-minded ruling body is organized. Next, the law reforms with structured enforcement polices, including small-weapons rearmament. In this growing city of strangers, little acts of violence begin and doors are locked for the first time since the plague proper. People simply don't know one another and so don't trust one another without the comforting, machine-enforced buffer of social authority. It is now that Stu turns to Frannie and asks her if "people ever learn anything" (1149). It is now that Frannie answers with the non-response that once ended The Stand: "I don't know" (1149).

For the greatest irony in the year of the plague is that most people—even God's minions—end where they began, needing institutions and wanting technology. And so, as this work closes out, its author leaves his readers with clear indications that most of those who escaped Captain Trips' clutches are drifting back within his reach. His name, finally, is more a metaphor for man's own folly than for disease. Inevitably, the dark man who was Randall Flagg is seen reborn again in the novel's epilogue, part of a wheel that only slows and never quite stops. All the defeat of organized evil can promise at the end of this epic is "A season of rest" (1149), a fallow time for King's holy family (Stu, Frannie, and the first post-plague baby, the sacred infant Peter) to escape the encroaching institutionalism and to grow by themselves in wisdom and grace. They will need both, for the plague will probably return as the wheel regains its impetus. Then it will be Peter (or some other chosen one) who will lead another band of survivors around the loop that circumvents the devil in man. The wheel and the loop may be part of God's plan, or they may be no more than the nature of the universe; but as circles, they never end, and The Stand suggests they never will.

WORKS CITED

Barker, Clive. "Surviving the Ride." Kingdom of Fear: The World of Stephen King. Ed. Tim Underwood and Chuck Miller, 1986. New York: HAL-Signet, 1987. 59-69.

King, Stephen. Danse Macabre. New York: Everest House, 1981. The Stand: The Complete and Uncut Edition. New York: Doubleday, 1990.

Magistrale, Tony. Landscape of Fear: Stephen King's American Gothic. Bowling Green, OH: Bowling Green State Univ. Popular Press, 1988.

Reino, Joseph. Stephen King: The First Decade, Carrie to Pet Sematary. Boston: Twayne, 1988.

Underwood, Tim, and Chuck Miller, eds. Bare Bones: Conversations on Terror with Stephen King. 1988. New York: Warner, 1989.

Winter, Douglas E. Stephen King: The Art of Darkness. New York: NAL, 1984.

Ziegler, Philip. The Black Death, 1969. New York: Harper & Row, 1971.

CHAPTER TWO

"I Think the Government Stinks!": Stephen King's <u>Stand</u> on Politics

Douglas Keesey

> Q: <u>The Stand</u> is very antigovernmental. Are those your personal feelings?
> KING: Oh, I think the government stinks! ... I believe what I wrote in <u>The Stand</u>. It always ends in one way. It's like taking dope or booze. You take enough government, and it's going to kill you. That's the end. Sooner or later it always goes down.
> —Stephen King in an interview, 1985 (Underwood, 88)

When the "complete and uncut" edition of <u>The Stand</u> was published in 1990, Stephen King wrote in the preface that he had simply restored material to the novel that had been cut from its 1978 edition. Readers could now enjoy <u>The Stand</u> "as it was originally written," "as its author originally intended for it to roll out of the showroom" (x,xii). But the 1990 model has some interesting new features on it, ones no designer ever dreamed back of in '78. Not only have many of the novel's dates been changed so that the apocalypse that was once due to hit us in the future (1985, from a 1978 perspective) is now upon us (1990), but the names of certain recent politicians have been added, most prominently those of Ronald Reagan (1981-88) and George Bush (1989-), as if to point the finger quite directly at those King considers to be inadequate leaders in this crucial period for deciding America's future. What was originally just a reference to Nixon's thirst for power gets expanded into an attack on Reagan's stupidity: "We used to watch Presidents decay before our very eyes from month to month and even week to week on national TV—except for Nixon, of course, who thrived on power the way that a vampire bat thrives on blood, *and*

21

Reagan, who seemed a little too stupid to get old" (630). (Italics mark the new material added to the 1990 edition.)

Sometimes King seems merely to be updating his political references, as when he describes a poster of "George Bush coming out of a church in Harlem, hands raised high, a big grin on his face. The caption, in huge red letters, said: YOU DON'T WANT TO LAY NO BOOGIE-WOOGIE ON THE KING OF ROCK AND ROLL!" (726). In the 1978 edition, Carter's name in where Bush's is now, and the implication is that both presidents—Democrat and Republican—were well-meaning but hopelessly ineffectual or, worse, merely putting on a campaign face in order to win election. Either way, they were not up to the task of true leadership. As Frannie thinks, referring to the superflu plague, an experimental in germ warfare that got out of hand: "They sure laid some boogie-woogie on you." Sometimes the negative attitude toward America's most recent leaders seems filtered through a potentially unreliable narrator. When Starkey, a representative of the military establishment, describes Bush as "the miserable worm who had been masquerading as a Chief Executive since January 20, 1989" (130), we may feel that we should take the character's possible bias into account and not simply equate King's opinion with Starkey's.

But what are we to think when King has a character whose perceptions we trust, Larry Underwood, describes Bush as the quintessential glad-hander, a selfishly devious politician like Harold Lauder?: "Larry's hand was pumped up and down exactly three times [by Harold] and let go. It reminded Larry of the time he had shaken hands with George Bush back when 'the old bushwacker' had been running for President" (686-687). Note that Harold does indeed try to ambush (bushwhack) Stu Redman and kill him. Recall that Harold is a front for, and a dupe of, the devil (Randall Flagg). It's not hard to see that the way Bush is described and the comparison with Harold imply a rather negative attitude on King's part toward the nation's 41st president. The 1978 edition has "Henry (Scoop) Jackson" where George Bush's name is now—and of course no reference to "bushwhacking."

It appears that when King reread his manuscript for the new edition, he couldn't help substituting a more current and powerfully relevant example of political deviousness. The fact that King has conducted this anti-Reagan and anti-Bush campaign on the sly, making no mention of this tendentious updating in his preface to the new edition, is no reason for us to discount it as mere tomfoolery. Indeed, the targeting of Reagan and Bush is right in line with the entire novel's suspicion, criticism, and eventual rejection of politics.

We have started at the end of the story, with King's revision for the 1990 edition, his naming of names which sharpens the novel as a political critique. Now let us return to the beginning, because the novel was, from its very conception, always political. Inspiration for The Stand came from three seemingly unrelated real-life events: a chemical-biological spill in Utah, the 1970s energy crisis, and the Patty Hearst affair. These events came together in King's mind in complex ways, and I present a greatly simplified version here. King associated the product of germ warfare experiments with the Symbionese Liberation Army that had kidnapped and brainwashed Patter Hearst: "I began by seeing this germ symbolically visualized in the SLA" (King, Danse Macabre, 374). The former represents destructive right-wing (military-industrial complex) activity and the latter, destructive leftist activity. When left and right become so polarized, there is little room for compromise: the two sides fight and destroy each other. In King's mind, a version of this struggle between political extremists was being played out every day as people fought in gas-station lines over what little gas there was to fill their tanks—and entire nations seemed on the brink of nuclear war over the energy crisis: "it seemed as if the whole world might go up in a series of fireballs over a lack of premium unleaded gasoline" (961).

In The Stand, King took this mid-70s real-life situation to its logical conclusion. Nuclear war doesn't occur, but a deadly germ— the superflu—spills out. The military and the government, embarrassed that their paranoid attempt to defend the country from leftist/communist attack has resulted in the very destruction they feared, try to evade responsibility for the disaster. They spread the germ to other countries so that it cannot be traced to America, thus making the disease even harder to fight. They kill those immune to the superflu in order to stop news of the disaster from getting out, thus passing up the chance to learn how to prevent the disease. And they lie to people— and to themselves—about the severity of the disease until it is too late really to do anything about it.

In the first part of The Stand, King gives readers an education in right-wing political irresponsibility and left-wing extremist reaction. Although set in 1990 (or 1985), The Stand recapitulates key events of the '60's, most notable the Kent State massacre, as King takes readers through the same political education he himself had recently undergone. King may deplore the destructive violence of revolutionary leftist groups like the SLA, but he understands that desperate acts which people sometimes feel driven to commit when they are betrayed by their government. In a 1980 interview, King traced his anger at the government back to the '60's and what he calls his own "political pilgrimage":

> I've always lived in Maine. I come from Anglo-Saxon stock. We're all Republicans. Dinosaurs walked the earth, my people were Republicans. One of the reasons I wanted to write a novel about Patty Hearst and the Symbionese Liberation Army was because I understood this upheaval they'd gone through. One of those little girls who was killed in the L.A. shoot-out worked for Goldwater in 1964. I worked for Goldwater in '64. I voted for Nixon in '68. I was convinced that people who burned their draft cards were yellow-bellies. My idea was, "Let's bomb 'em into the Stone Age." I went to college from 1966 to 1970, and it was an accretion of the facts—teaching, seminars, and little by little I came around. It's like someone who converts . . .

Q: You became a zealot.
KING: That's right. And the marches and everything else followed. (Underwood, 99)

In The Stand, King has Dr. Soames, among other characters, realize that young people's fear of the government, expressed most openly during the '60s, was justified: the military-industrial complex was experimenting with germ warfare, in direct violation of Geneva accords, and the technology got out of control. As Dr. Soames says, "I used to be frightened of the younger generation's paranoia, do you know that? Always afraid someone was tapping their phones . . . following them . . . running computer checks on them . . . and now I find out they were right and I was wrong" (151). At Kent State, students trying to attract attention to the truth about the superflu's deadliness and the government's lies are shot down by soldiers, as if the year were 1970 instead of 1990 and the protests were against the Vietnam War instead of germ warfare.

But King's novel does not merely portray the political left as innocent victims of the right's unjustified aggression. King follows certain characters through to the stage that he himself once occupied (if only intellectually), that of the left-wing "zealot" whose extremism is an equal and opposite reaction to right-wing persecution. One example of such a character is Brother Zeno, formerly Sergeant First Class Roland Gibbs, who breaks from the ranks of the U.S. Army and, in revulsion at the cruelty and stupidity of those in power, sets himself up as leader in their place. But, in reacting against right-wing violence, Brother Zeno becomes a mirror of that violence, as aggressively paranoid and as intolerant of dissent as his former masters: "I . . . proclaim myself first President of the Republic of Northern California! We are in control! We are in control! If you officers in the field try to countermand my orders, shoot them like dogs in the street! . . . Take down name, rank, and serial numbers of deserters! . . . A new day is dawning! The day of the oppressor is ended!" (225). Brother Zeno forgets that he himself was recently a deserter from the regular army and that

25

he left for what he felt were good reasons. In the extremity of his re-action against oppression, Brother Zeno becomes the new oppressor. As a black revolutionary, Brother Zeno is "a Klu Klux Klansman's worst nightmare of headhunting Africans" (224), but in playing the part of the headhunter written for him by the fears of powerful whites, Brother Zeno becomes a mere extension of right-wing white hatred—left-wing black hatred. Brother Zeno is clearly King's negative com-ment on some of the more violent members of the '60's black power movement, related to the Symbionese Liberation Army in terms of their ideological extremism and the ruthless pursuit of their goals.

Though generally more sympathetic to the left than to the right, King's attitude toward extremist groups on both side is summed up in his suggestion that they are being mislead by the devil: their passion-ate beliefs are being perverted into destructive actions by unscrupu-lous men like Randall Flagg, who is interested in power, not principles. Flagg stirs up white resentment at a poverty and unemployment until it becomes virulent racism, *and* Flagg incites the righteous indigna-tion of persecuted blacks into retaliatory violence: "He and a black veteran of Nam—the black had more than enough hate to make up for his missing left leg—had offed six cops in New York and New Jer-sey. In Georgia he was Ramsey Forrest, a distant descendant of Nathan Bedford Forrest, and in his white sheet he had participated in two rapes, a castration, and the burning of a nigger shanty town" (183). Flagg encourages the military-industrial complex to develop powerful weap-ons against communism, like deadly chemicals, so that he can use them. He incites radical groups like the Symbionese Liberation Army to kidnap rich men's daughters so that he himself can gain more of their power. Flagg is and "equal opportunity reader" (181), a carrier of left- and right-wing propaganda, a believer in all causes—as long as they further his own goals. In Randall Flagg King has created a fig-ure for the egotism and hatred at the root of all political extremism.

By the mid-70s, King has reached a third stage in the evolu-tion of his political understanding. Having been radicalized by groups that pointed out to him how dangerous and irresponsible the government was being (the chemical-biological spill in Utah), he had since been repelled by the violence committed by some of those radical groups (the SLA kidnapping of Patty Hearst). Whereas before it might have been natural for King to associate a deadly form of germ only with his government (the military-industrial complex that produced it), now it became as natural for King to link this germ and its spreading destruction with SLA and other revolutionary *left*-wing groups. What King saw was an increasing exacerbation of the war between ideologically polarized movements, and, with the energy crisis only raising the tension, no political solution to the problem seemed in sight. Indeed, "politics" itself, which always appeared to bring with it dichotomous thinking—one was either on the left or on the right—seemed to be a large part of the problem.

Frustrated at the violence of both the left and the right, exhausted by the very problem of the dichotomy between them, King decided to destroy everyone and their problems—but only in fantasy, in a book—and not quite everyone. Still, King's destructive action—having all those characters die from a germ, the superflu, he created—was enough like the apocalyptic violence he deplored in left- and right-wing extremist groups to make King nervous about what he had done. King knew that in writing The Stand he had succumbed to the same desperate urge for an immediate solution to difficult problems that had led so many political extremists to commit violence, and he also knew that his own destructive action, like theirs, was largely a power trip:

> You see, I began to see the energy crisis as just one domino in a complex economic structure that was going to go down completely. The more I thought about this particular Gordian knot, the more I thought, "Suppose everybody died except maybe a certain percentage of the world's population—then there'd be enough oil!" . . . The Stand was particularly fulfilling, because there I got a chance to scrub the whole human race and, man, it was fun! Sitting

the typewriter, I felt just like Alexander lifting his sword over the Gordian knot and snarling, "Fuck unraveling it; I'll do it *my* way!"

Much of the compulsive, driven feeling I had while I worked on the The Stand came from the vicarious thrill of imagining an entire entrenched social order destroyed in one stroke. That's the mad-bomber side of my character, I suppose. (Underwood, 30, 98)

In Greek mythology, an oracle stated that he who untied the Gordian knot would rule all of Asia; rather than unravel it, Alexander took the more direct and violent route to a (dis)solution. In cutting through the knot that represents society's problems—but only because he's killed the people along with their problems—King has indeed acted (in fantasy) like a "mad bomber." Here we might think that King is implicitly likening himself to such left-wing extremist groups as the Weathermen, who were known to bomb public buildings as part of their revolutionary activities. But note that King also uses the "Gordian knot" analogy in The Stand in a passage which, together with the statement above, implies that he and the military-industrial complex are both equally guilty of releasing the superflu plague: "it was the people in authority who did this. They're good at putting things back in order. They've solved the depressed economy, pollution, the oil shortage, and the cold ware, all at a stroke. Yeah, they put things in order, all right. They solved everything the same way Alexander solved the Gordian knot—by cutting it in two with his sword" (225). My point is that King knew from inside the passionate frustration at the world's problems that drives the left- and right-wingers alike to seek quick, violent solutions.

But the destruction wreaked by extremist groups and by the superflu plague is, of course, only one side of the The Stand. Once King has cut the Gordian knot of "an entire entrenched social order," he proceeds to explore the possibility the creation of a new society.

28

Will the survivors simply retie the knot and provoke someone to cut it again, this time perhaps leaving no survivors at all, or will they take advantage of their second change and create a less polarized, more peaceful civilization? If the superflu marked "the end of all hope in our government" (215), could there now be another, better government in its place? Gradually, the various survivors scattered across the country after the superflu disaster form groups which join other, even larger groups, eventually converging in Boulder, Colorado. Chapters of the novel which were once short and disjointed grow longer and become coordinated with other chapters as characters meet and find community, linking up with others who share their formerly disparate perspectives. In order to ensure that they will continue to see eye to eye, people select a committee to make laws for the Free Zone, laws that reinstate the best of past society: its Constitution and Bill of Rights. The ideal is now, as it was then, to preserve a balance between social order and individual freedom.

But this new society is soon face to face with some very old problems; the new government becomes embroiled in many of the same politics as the old. Let us consider these problems in the order in which they are presented in the novel, calling them, for convenience, (1) internal, (2) external, and (3) internal-external.

(1) Internal problems. When Glen and Stu get together, they decide that the people can't be trusted to know what's best for their own good. Rather than democracy, the people might decide they want a theocracy or a dictatorship: "We want—we *need*—to catch them before they wake up an do something nutty" (648). So, in order to get the new democracy going Glen and Stu decide to "short-circut the democratic process" (649): they rig the election by handpicking people who will nominate them and their friends as the Free Zone's leaders. In addition, Nick furthers the "leadership coup" by using tricks to "misdirect" attention away from Harold as a potential candidate for leadership (668): rather than let the people decide, Nick makes the decision for them that Harold is unfit. As Nick realizes, this shining new society has some "dirty" "*Politics*" at its core (669, 668); it is compromised right from the start.

Further compromises come when the Free Zone leaders decide that not they themselves, but three other citizens should be the ones to go on a dangerous mission as spies to Las Vegas, Flagg's stronghold. The Free Zone Committee reasons (or rationalizes) that these citizens are not only better equipped to by spies, but also more expendable than any of the members of the Committee. But, as Fran points out, the practice of spying and the habit it sending other people to do their leaders' dirty work are characteristics of the old, pre-plague government. Such paranoid suspicion of "the enemy" and disregard for the safety of one's own citizens are what led to the superflu disaster in the first place: "Don't any of you understand that's the same as starting all the old shit over again?" (713). King leaves open the question of whether or not the end justifies the means in this case: are the Committee's "dirty" politics and acts necessary to the founding and defense of the new society, or do they hopelessly weaken that society by compromising the democratic principles it supposedly stands for? The Committee members do wrestle with their consciences, and one spy does end up bringing important information about Flagg to the Committee, but King leaves us wondering to what extent the Free Zone has sold its soul for physical safety. Internally, the Free Zone has paid a high moral price for its preservation from threatening external forces.

(2) External problems. While the Free Zone Committee is trying not to become a dictatorship in its very effort to combat Flagg's dictatorship, trying not to mirror Flagg's (and the previous government's) paranoid suspicion of and violence toward "the enemy," Flagg himself is taking advantage of the moral scruples that prevent the Free Zone Committee from taking decisive action against him. Harold, as one of Flagg's disciples, proves even more adept than the Committee at manipulating the way people in the Free Zone vote, because Harold has no guilty conscience to slow him down. Harold uses dirty politics to evil ends; he compromises democracy in order to destroy it: "When he had finished with them they wouldn't even have had a fucking quorum left" (736). Unable to leave behind grudges he developed in

the pre-plague years to make a fresh start, Harold believes, like most resentful men, that the world is a dog-eat-dog place where only the fittest survive:

"While you are meditating on the beauties of constitutional rule, spare a little time to meditate on Randall Flagg, Man of the West. I doubt very much if he has any time to spare for such fripperies as public meetings and ratifications and discussions on the true meaning of a peach in the best literal mode. Instead he has been concentrating on the basics, on his Darwin, preparing to wipe the great Formica counter of the universe with your dead bodies." (829)

Harold may not see the extent to which his belief in a cruel world is what makes that world cruel, but, for those who are the object of his hatred, that doesn't matter: whether Harold is effect or cause of a cruel world, he is out to get them.

Does King think that the Free Zone Committee and its constitution are any match for conscienceless Harold and Randall Flagg? Is it possible for democracy ("public meetings and ratifications and discussions") to fight evil effectively? An early sense of King's answer to this question comes from the divinely inspired Leo, who warns Larry that "The Committee won't help you, it won't help anyone, the committee is the old way, *he* [Flagg] laughs at your committee because it's the old way, and the old ways are *his* ways" (858). But didn't The Stand bring all these good people together in Boulder, Colorado so that they could form a new society, elect a Committee of leaders, re-ratify the Constitution and the Bill of Rights? Hasn't the novel been all about giving democracy a second chance, this time maybe to conquer internal and external evil?

Actually, though at times it may seem to be the case, that is not what the novel has been about. As Mother Abagail reminds the Committee members (and King's readers), "God didn't bring you folks together to make a committee or a community . . . He brought you here

31

only to send you further, on a quest. He means for you to try and destroy this Dark Prince, this Man of Far Leagues" (917). Thus, rather late in the novel, the search for political solutions to society's problems gives way to a quest narrative, in which four men, formerly members of the Free Zone Committee, leave all public meetings and ratifications and discussions behind to go forth as individuals to confront evil. Rather than a democracy, the Free Zone proves to be a theocracy after all, with the divinely inspired Mother Abagail dictating the terms—the *only* terms by which the Free Zone can successfully do battle with Randall Flagg. The Stand is about the failure of democratic politics to solve the world's problems, and the necessity for heroic individual (and divinely inspired) action to defeat evil. The Free Zone cannot make its stand in the town meeting hall of Boulder, Colorado. No, as Mother Abagail makes clear, Randall Flagg "is in Las Vegas, and you must go there, and it is there that you will make you stand" (919).

It might be tempting to think of The Stand as a book about faith in religion and in politics, but in fact the novel dramatically chooses one over the other. As Mother Abagail says (and everything about the end of The Stand seems to support her), "I sinned in pride. So have you all, all sinned in pride. Ain't you heard it said, put not your faith in the lords and princes of this world?" (917). Indeed, we have heard this said, but mostly about the pre-plague government, as when Fran's father used to tell her, "You had to trust yourself . . . and let the princes of this world get along as best they could with the people who has elected them. Most times that wasn't very well, but that was okay; they deserved each other" (53). But Fran, as a Free Zone Committee member, was to be part of a new and better government, and we are surprised to hear Mother Abagail talking about the Free Zone Committee using the same words that once described the old government. The fact is that King seems unwilling to put his faith in any government. Whether the Free Zone has to weak a conscience to avoid becoming corrupt like the previous government, or whether its moral scruples are too strong to enable it to defeat Flagg through democratic means, it's clear that King does not trust the Committee as a defense against evil.

To trust in democratic politics, in the work of a committee, is to believe that humans can discuss, debate, and reason their way to a solution to the world's problems. But King does not believe that humans know enough about the world to enable them to do this. For the members of the Free Zone Committee to think that they can figure out through public debate the solution to society's problems is to commit the sin of pride: they have put too much faith in their own rational understanding. This is the one mistake that the pre-plague government made: it too tried to make politics work, and look what happened—the devastating superflu. As Glen explains, in what may well be the most important passage in The Stand:

> "Rationalism is the idea we can ever understand anything about the state of being. It's a deathtrip. It always has been. so you can charge the superflu off to rationalism if you want. But the other reason we're here [in Boulder] is the dreams, and the dreams are *irrational*. We've agreed not to talk about that simple fact while we're in committee, but we're not in committee now. So, I'll say what we all know is true: We're here under the fiat of powers we don't understand. For me, that means we may be beginning to accept—only subconsciously now, and with plenty of slips backward due to culture lag—a different definition of existence. The idea that we can never understand *anything* about the state of being. And if rationalism is a deathtrip, then irrationalism might very well be a lifetrip . . . at least unless it proves otherwise." (741)

Discussion of dreams (of Mother Abagail, of Randall Flagg) has no place in committee meetings, where the leaders of the Free Zone are rationally trying to solve society's problems. Unfortunately, this belief in rationalism is what caused those problems in the first place! This Free Zone needs less trust in rational politics and more faith in irrational dreams: they must listen to Mother Abagail when she tells them that committees are not the answer; only individual action guided by religious faith can save the world. If King believes that there is some way to combine individual faith and democratic politics, The Stand doesn't show it. In fact, it shows the opposite, which we might repeat for emphasis here in Leo's and Mother Abagail's divinely inspired words: "The committee won't help you, it won't help anyone, the committee is the old way [rationalism], *he* laughs at you committee because it's the old way and the old ways are *his* ways . . . God didn't bring you folks together to make a committee or a community . . . put not your faith in the lords and princes of this world" (848, 971).

(3) Internal/external problems. After the fiery finale of The Stand, in which Flagg's rationalism proves self-defeating and former Committee members Larry and Ralph, through individual action and irrational faith, triumph over evil, the rest of The Stand may seem anticlimactic. But is important to see that The Stand's ending represents the logical extension of King's rejection of politics. The surviving Committee members, Stu and Fran, resign from the Committee and leave political life behind forever. Now that the population of the Free Zone has grown so big, many people are strangers to each other. The problem of potentially threatening outsiders was not solved by the destruction of Flagg and his followers; instead, the problem has come inside: any one of the growing Free Zone population could be a potential new Flagg. In order to ensure order among so many strangers, the Free Zone Committee has now authorized deputies to carry guns. Whether or not these weapons will help solve or only exacerbate the problem of violence remains an open question, but Stu suspects that society, by being so aggressively defensive, is once again turning into the mirror image of the destructive-

ness it claims to deplore. By relying on rationalism to solve society's problems, politicians only make them worse. It becomes increasingly difficult to tell internal from external problems: is "the enemy" the stranger sitting next to you, or is it a part of yourself, the part that would kill for fear of being killed?

In Fran and Stu's resignation from the Free Zone Committee and in their withdrawal from an increasingly populous society, we can see King's final comment on the futility of politics and his distrust of any rational attempt to organize society, no matter how well intended. The novel's final image for such attempts at organization is that of cancer: "As [Stu] followed [Fran] inside Mother Abagail's house he thought it would be better, much better, if they did break down and spread. Postpone organization as long as possible. It was organization that always seemed to cause the problem. When the cells began to clump together and grow dark" (1148). Mother Abagail would have approved if this comparison of politics to cancer. The superflu plague was like cancer, and it resulted from politics, from rationalism. If King sees a hope for the future, it is clear that he does not look for it in politics. When the time comes to take a stand against evil, only faith in the irrational will do.

WORKS CITED

King, Stephen. <u>Danse Macabre</u>. New York: Everest House, 1981. <u>The Stand</u>. New York: Doubleday, 1990.

Underwood, Tim, and Chuck Miller, eds. <u>Bare Bones: Conversations on Terror with Stephen King</u>. New York: McGraw-Hill, 1988.

CHAPTER THREE

Stephen King and His Readers: A Dirty, Compelling Romance

Brian Kent

Whose Stephen King is this Anyhow?

When Stephen King's Needful Things appeared in 1991, reviewer Joe Queenan, feeling no obligation to mask his contempt for The Stephen King Phenomenon, dismissed it as "the literary equivalent of heavy metal" (King must have smiled). "It is not," Queenan sneered, "the sort of book that one can readily recommend to the dilettante, to the dabbler or to anyone with a reasonable-sized brain. It is the type of book that can be enjoyed only by longtime aficionados of the genre, people who probably have a lot of black T-shirts in their chest of drawers and either have worn or have dreamed of wearing a baseball cap backward." And the reason King's novel is so unrecommendable to civilized ladies and gents? It is peopled "with ultra low-rollers—couch potatoes, barmy widows, small-time hoods—rarely producing a character that an intelligent, *normal* [emphasis his] reader could identify with, much less like" (13). No doubt, Queenan himself is the prototype for this reader's Everyman.

Not surprisingly, a few weeks later the New York Times Book Review, where the above ran, carried a couple of letters rebutting Mr. Queenan's assessment of King. The first respondent began by making it clear she is "a well-educated individual who reads Voltaire, Colette, and Flaubert" (before going on to make an analogy between King and potato chips). The second offered a spirited defense of King's reliance on popular culture, then closed with the following declaration: "I do not have a chest of drawers stuffed with a lot of black T-shirts, and I have never worn or dreamed of wearing a baseball cap backward" ("Letters," 54).

Anyone familiar with the critical reaction to Stephen King's novels will recognize Queenan's snottiness as a regular feature (although others have achieved it with a great deal more panache). What's interesting about the critical jousting outlined above is the pose offered by King's defenders—they appear to validate Queenan's belief that the black T-shirt crowd is beneath consideration as a legitimate literary audience. From the tone of their letters, one might guess that both correspondents, although they might reluctantly acknowledge that King does indeed attract a "heavy metal" readership, would not care to find themselves sitting on the subway beside an individual member of that readership—headphoned skull bouncing from shoulder to shoulder, Bazooka balloon rising on the hot air of marijuana exhaust—sharing in the pleasures of a King paperback scarefest. They may be out there, but My God! they have nothing to do with *me*.

This latest episode in the ever-escalating skirmish over the merits of Stephen King's fiction, puts me in mind of a review that appeared in The Nation upon publication of Bobbie Ann Mason's In Country in 1986. The novel, which centers on a young girl's coming to grips with both adulthood and her father having been killed in Vietnam before she was born, is written in a minimalist vein. It also incorporates many of the pop culture elements so often noted in King's work (TV, movies, pop music, advertising, brand names). In Country is stylish, but in an unstylish way, and is accessible to any reader past the sixth grade. In reviewing the book, Mona Molarsky hit on a telling conundrum that is equally valid for much of King's fiction: "Mason's exploration of the ways in which popular culture can either encourage or challenge naiveté is an ambitious project and one not without its problems. While remaining true to the spirit of Sam's character, Mason must paint a backdrop wide yet detailed enough to offer a complex vision" (58).

Molarsky expanded on this observation by telling the story of six years she had spent watching her young female next-door neighbor grow up in Plainfield, New Jersey, where "a happy ending ... is when you stay out of trouble, get a job, get married, and buy a microwave oven." Her young neighbor, Kirsten, appeared in many respects to *be* Samantha Hughes, the protagonist of Mason's novel. Molarsky concluded: "Ironically, the people Mason seems to care most about are the ones least likely to read her book. One recent Sunday I brought Kirsten a copy of In Country. Would she recognize the characters, I wondered? That was weeks ago, and the book is still sitting where I left it—next to the TV, which is always on. Whose literature is this anyhow?" (58). Good question. And an especially compelling one when it comes to King, since he more than any other contemporary novelist reaches the Kirstens out there (what the trade refers to as the "non-book audience"), pulling them away from their TVs and Walkmans and engaging them in the act of reading for pleasure. He does this, no less, while retaining those readers whom Darrell Schweitzer refers to as an "influential, but numerically small, audience of people who read a lot and have taste" (5). King's broad appeal is as remarkable an achievement as literature has produced in recent memory.

But these two camps of King devotees remain pretty distinct. In one are those who have fostered what is consistently referred to in the King literature as a growing cottage industry of works about King and about his books. For the most part, these folks are very protective of their Stevie, and by the very nature of their activities (writing and reading critical books and articles, establishing newsletters, responding to book reviews) one cultural step removed from the other camp (something they are often eager to point out).

In the other, a much larger but far less professional body of readers, are the millions of people who pick up a book (perhaps only occasionally, and in some cases only when a new King hits the bookstores), read it, maybe discuss it informally with friends or mates, put it on a bookshelf or trade it in at the Exchange, and then go about their daily routines. They feel no compulsion to offer, for example, detailed analyses of King's intentions, nor do they have an overwhelming desire to contact "America's literary boogeyman" personally. They don't all wear black T-shirts and baseball caps (backward or forward), but some do. They are average Americans—store clerks, factory workers, doctors, lawyers, you name it. *Normal* people, you might say (even if Mr. Queenan would not).

Far removed from the literary snobs so wonderfully defined by Queenan's review of Needful Things, one might call these readers literary slobs. And I don't mean that in a pejorative sense. But just as your garden variety slob goes about his messy business unmindful of the social conventions governing personal hygiene, or good housekeeping, or dinner table etiquette, the literary slob pursues his reading pleasures without an iota of concern for what critical theory is currently carrying the day in the halls of academe, or what social significance is inherent in the particular manifestations of King's monsters, or even why King and not someone else has managed to so successfully engage him in a tale. A likable lot, literary slobs. And I suspect King's heart (if not always his mind) goes out to this segment of his audience more so than the first.

Most writers who approach King from a favorable point of view echo Schweitzer's amazement over King's ability to reach such a large and broad-based audience, while maintaining a dedicated coterie of more scholarly-academic readers. I think the more accurate statement of his remarkable accomplishment is that he has carved out a sizable audience of scholarly-academic readers, while maintaining and expanding his massive popular appeal. For while his heart may be with that huge popular audience, his mind often lands him in academic terrain, in terms of his own awareness of the standards and skills around which university English departments cohere. Stephen King is a highly educated—through formal university training and his own voracious reading habits—student of literature. So as much as he likes to trumpet the primacy of telling a good story, as though that were his only concern and he is content to sit atop the bestseller lists with, for example, the current number one—Alexandra Ripley and her sequel to Gone With the Wind, he is clearly uncomfortable keeping such company. And well he should be.

King can write to please university professors if he chooses, and he often chooses, but his special gift is his ability to use the tools of sophisticated literary construction in such a way that the literary slobs who constitute the bulk of his readership are not put off or intimidated and still get the point. Their predominant impression remains that King is one of them. Sometimes this means sacrificing subtlety or finesse, to the chagrin of literary detectives burning with the desire to put their 20-some odd years of schooling to the test, but King willingly makes that sacrifice in order to successfully convey something about literary conventions, or historical and contemporary allusions, or bodies of knowledge outside the realm of his readers' everyday experiences. And he does this while never losing track of his first concern—the story.

King manages this without alienating his mass audience, I think, because he has somehow retained a deep, empathic understanding of what brings people to books at the earliest of ages or despite the least sophisticated of educations, so he never makes readers feel belittled or stupid for not getting his point or for needing help getting his point. This no doubt has a lot to do with his own background and his own self-fueled drive down what one reviewer has termed the road "from Road Runner to Raskolnikov" (Solomon, 21). So, far from denigrating or feeling contemptuous of the black T-shirted among his readers, King befriends them with a "Come here, I've got something to show you" (one can almost hear Megadeath thrashing in the background and sniff a case of stale Bud empties in the foreground), gets their attention, keeps it, and might even educate them along the way to some finer points of literary appreciation.

Which brings me to The Stand. King's long novel of the struggle between good and evil in post-apocalyptic America ranks as a favorite among his fans. King says so himself in the Preface to the Complete and Uncut Edition. As such, it is a good vehicle for exploring the issues discussed above to see how they play out in the fiction. The Stand is especially appropriate for another reason as well. Its central plot device of a plague that wipes out 98% of America's (and the world's) population emphasizes the dangers of pursuing too rational a course—as King writes, "At the end of all rationalism, the mass grave" (741). He counters rationalism with what Glen Bateman calls White Magic (Douglas Winter terms it "faith in faith" [72]), which incorporates elements of rationality, but not to the exclusion of more emotionally-based perceptions and beliefs. The novel's affirmation of faith, of magic, takes on a decidedly anti-academic cast, since King implies that the academy worships rationality as the basis for all true progress and enlightenment. For ordinary citizens outside the realm where important, potentially catastrophic, decisions are made concerning the very nature of their lives, this anti-academic stance hits home—and sustains the belief that King, as author, is someone they can trust.

Plain Fiction for Plain Folks

Following the recent death of Michael Landon, Entertainment Weekly ran a piece evaluating Landon's television career that zeroed in on an essential characteristic of his work:

> Knocking Landon's shows is like complaining that Mom, the American flag, and apple pie are clichéd; the complaint is true but nearly irrelevant, because lots of people *like* clichés, and lots of people is what mass entertainment is all about. Landon came to his work *free of cynicism* [emphasis added]. As a craftsman inspired and excited by the most common dramatic story lines and plot twists, he could thrive in television, producing one hit after another. (Tucker 45)

King brings a similar cynicism-free outlook to his fiction, especially in regard to the ordinary activities of ordinary people, and thus avoids trivializing the mundane. King's literary perspective is essentially void of the soul-killing irony so endemic to contemporary America, especially in the arts. He demonstrates a humility that allows him to be, in his fiction, just "a hick from Maine" (to borrow his own words). Readers latch on to this sensibility, seeing in it an authentic voice for their own lives.

An early scene in The Stand highlights this authentic quality. In Chapter 3, Lila Bruett, baby-sitting at Sally and Ralph Hodges' house and enjoying her soaps on their color TV, surveys her surroundings:

> Lila let her eyes drift around the room and wished her own house looked this nice. Sally's hobby was doing paint-by-the-numbers pictures of Christ, and they were all over the living room in nice frames. She especially liked the big one of the Last Supper mounted in back of the TV; it had come with sixty different oil colors, Sally had told her, and it took almost three months to finish. It was a real work of art. (27)

The situation is ripe for a snidely ironic caricature of these lower middle class lives, but King plays it straight. There's not a hint of irony or contempt either for Sally's love of her paint-by-numbers religious artifacts or for Lila's appreciation of them as works of art. King allows them their own sensibilities and perceptions without imposing an authorial judgment on them. In short, he accords the characters *respect*. That same respect carries over into readers' understanding the scene. King doesn't look down at readers as the all-knowing, all-seeing, all-judging AUTHOR, but instead seems to inhabit whatever circle of circumstances they themselves occupy.

This characteristic lays King open for critical abuse when the circle of circumstances he inhabits calls for crassness or vulgarity, something he seems particularly comfortable with and adept at. When King puts words into characters' mouths such as Fran's playful rejoinder to Stu—"You may be a Founding Father and all that, but you still leave an occasional skidmark in your underdrawers" (694), he does so not to poke fun at their inelegant manner, but because he knows this is how people talk and think. For that, King himself is deemed an inelegant clod and his readers presumed to be illiterate TV-zombies. Queenan's black T-shirt jibe is typical of the disdain more (one assumes) sophisticated readers frequently harbor toward King, and especially toward his readers. John Podhoretz, reviewing *It*, described King's prose in parts as "real get-down-in-the-gutter-and-sound-like-an-illiterate-moron-writing" (qtd. in Collings, 71). Andy Solomon's review of *Four Past Midnight* bemoaned the fact that in one instance five pages are devoted to "more detail than we care for to describe a man's getting interrupted in the bathroom by a phone call" (21).

Critics may continually chastise King for lapses in taste, but even they must often begrudgingly admit that he displays a candor in these moments that disarms criticism. Don Herron, for example, somewhat skeptically concludes that King's "characters swear. They excrete. They often act crudely, grossly. The hotrodder Billy Nolan in *Carrie* is described as having the 'unfailing ability to pinpoint the vulgar.' King has this ability in spades, and uses it often. It is a kind of honesty, and I suspect it is one of his greatest commercial aspects" (89). Peter Straub sees this ability as King working "with the real stuff of the world" (9), and in the same way as Straub suggests King had "shown [him] how to escape from [his] own education" (10), average readers view King's ability to pinpoint the vulgar as a recognition, and a validation, of their lives and behavior. Without doubt, it makes King's fiction more commercial. But it also allows King more freedom to open up the possibilities of fiction to his readers, because it garners their trust.

In *The Stand*, Stu Redman best personifies King's knack for instilling characters with ordinary human characteristics. Winter sees in Redman "a celebration of ordinary human existence" (65-66). It is no accident that Redman is the lone survivor of the group that travels across the desert to confront the Dark Man. He represents what is good and decent in ordinary citizens—unknowingly, without pretense. When Stu is on the road after making his escape from Stovington, he gets homesick for old friends and acquaintances. The nature of his reverie at this point reveals a great deal about his character:

> The thoughts that came wanted to be wholly
> good. Going hunting at dawn, bundled up in quilted

jackets and Day-Glo orange vests. Poker games at Ralph Hodges' house and Willy Craddock always complaining about how he was four dollars in the game, even if he was twenty ahead. Six or seven of them pushing Tony Leominster's Scout back onto the road that time he went down into the ditch drunk out of his mind, Tony staggering around and swearing to God and all the saints that he had swerved to avoid a U-Haul full of Mexican wetbacks. Jesus, how they had laughed. Chris Ortega's endless stream of ethnic jokes. Going down to Huntsville for whores, and that time Joe Bob Brentwood caught the crabs and tried to tell everybody they came from the sofa in the parlor and not from the girl upstairs. They had been goddamn good times. Not what your sophisticates with their nightclubs and their fancy restaurants and their museums would think of as good times, maybe, but good times just the same. (387)

To say that Stu Redman is a good and decent man is not to say he's perfect, as portions of this passage reveal. Nevertheless, Stu's thoughts detail the simple joys of a life lived far from the fast lane. Generally speaking, "your sophisticates" are not where King aims his literary canons. He doesn't begrudge them coming along, but it has to be on his terms, as crass, as vulgar, as sentimental, and as clichéd as those terms may turn out to be. In The Art of Darkness, Douglas Winter tells of King's participation in an undergraduate poetry seminar at the University of Maine-Orono. In it King encountered the concept of "white soul" from his instructor Burton Hatlen. The question Hatlen posed to his students was "Is there such a thing as white soul? suburban soul?" King's reaction says a lot about his relationship to the kind of readers Stu Redman represents: "Something in all that reached out to me, because I liked McDonald's and Dairy Queen and things like that. You'd see people bopping in there, and it seemed to me they did

45

have white soul" (Winter, 24). It's the kind of belief that unselfconsciously demonstrates that King's respect for "ordinary human existence" is born of his own experience growing up in rural Maine. One can also see in it the seed that will grow into King's later (and more self-conscious) explanation for his success: "Most of [my novels] have been plain fiction for plain folks, the literary equivalent of a Big Mac and a large fries from McDonald's" (Afterword, 524).

Growing up in a small Maine town, in a single parent household, not knowing his father, and under what he calls lower middle class circumstances, King might well feel a natural kinship with the unsophisticated herd rather than the more refined elite. In King's case, it appears that kinship was not educated out of him at the University of Maine, perhaps due to his own stubborn persistence not to let it be. Chris Chesley, one of King's boyhood friends in Durham, Maine, and thus someone with a unique perspective from which to view King's link to the culturally disenfranchised, has astutely placed King within the context of contemporary literature:

> Steve was by no means nurtured as a writer by the heritage of middle-class America—as the American middle class likes to see itself, that is. He was influenced by a working class, gritty little rural town. And in that sense it made him intellectually, and literally, an outsider. And I think a lot of the push, a lot of the drive, a lot of the narrative force in his writing stems directly from that—his sense of himself as being outside the mainstream, outside the American suburban middle class ethos.
>
> And that, in a way, is why I think many people are attracted to his writing—because it has the force, the stamina, and it has the vitality which American middle class writing doesn't have. (Spignesi, 50)

The irony of Chesley's appraisal is that King is rightly credited with bringing horror to the suburbs. But, again, on his own terms—

terms influenced by his being an outsider in the social and cultural sense Chesley describes, but also in a personal sense, of being "just sort of a nerdy kid." As King tells it, "I didn't get beat up too much because I was big, played a little football and stuff like that. So mostly I just got this 'King—he's weird. Big glasses. Reads a lot. Big teeth'" (Underwood and Miller, Kingdom, 65).

As a hugely successful author, King had left this background far behind him by the time he published The Stand in 1978. But he remained attuned to it on a deeply emotional level, even if his success had tinged that connection with a degree of ambiguity. When Larry Underwood meets up with Nadine and Joe on the Maine coast, he looks out on the tourist-inspired flavor of the coastline—"the essence of honky-tonk beach resort . . . gas stations, fried clam stands, Dairy Treets, motels painted in feverish pastel colors, mini-golf." In short, the basic accoutrements of an unsophisticated conception of daily life. King follows this with Larry's reaction to what he observes, a reaction that seems also an evocation of a now educated, wealthy, and famous author looking back on his past:

> Larry was drawn two painful ways by these things. Part of him clamored at their sad and blatant ugliness and at the ugliness of the minds that had turned this section of a magnificent, savage coastline into one long highway amusement park for families in station wagons. But there was a more subtle, deeper part of him that whispered of the people who had filled these places and this road during other summers. Ladies in sunhats and shorts too tight for their large behinds. College boys in red-and-black-striped rugby shirts. Girls in beach shifts and thong sandals. Small screaming children with ice cream spread over their faces. They were American people and there was a kind of dirty, compelling romance about them whenever they were in groups—never

mind if the group was in an Aspen ski lodge or performing their prosaic-arcane rites of summer along
US 1 in Maine. (458)

I believe it's the second of these two painful ways of viewing
things—the dirty, compelling romance—that keeps King attuned to
his mass audience, despite his intellectual awareness of other more
sophisticated, more refined sensibilities that can govern individual
lives, and certainly an economic situation far removed from the seedi-
ness implied in the scene above. It may prove a perspective increasingly difficult to hold on to for someone in King's position. But at least
up until now King has maintained a fundamental respect for those who
might well bear the brunt of an ironic or contemptuous display of "civilized" culture at the hands of other authors.

Follow Me, O Constant Reader

King doesn't rely just on his fiction to solidify his relationship
with readers. He keeps in regular contact with them through a
running, direct, one-sided conversation carried on in Introductions,
Forenotes, Afterwords, Headnotes, and various other nonfictional
and interview settings. The accumulation of these correspondences
amounts to the development of a bona fide literary persona, outside of the novels and short stories, that communicates in a
friendly, gracious, self-denigrating, down-to-earth, drinking-
buddy-type manner. The degree to which this persona reflects the
real King is impossible to gauge, but most readers are likely to
assume that the King they read in these instances is the King who
conducts his daily affairs in Bangor, Maine.

Tyson Blue claims the Stephen King literary persona gives
"readers a feeling that the writer is talking to them, and can even
make the reader come to feel he is coming to know the writer personally." Blue concludes, however, that "this is, of course, not the
case" (23). But regardless of whether the Stephen King who signs
his name and hometown at the end of these Introductions and
Afterwords is the same Stephen King who cashes his royalty

checks, there is no question but that the persona contributes a great deal to King's readers' perceptions of him and thus of his work. And the same goes for critics.

The 2-part Preface to the uncut version of The Stand offers a good sampling of the King persona. Part 1 opens graciously, King warning the potential buyer, whom he has come to affectionately call Constant Reader, that the current version of The Stand does not take the narrative "in an entirely new direction," and to save his money if that's what he expects. Once establishing this sense of fair play, King invites that buyer to "come along with me just a little farther. I have lots to tell you, and I think we can talk better around the corner. In the dark" (ix-x). The personal link between author and reader is forged.

That initial task complete, King later reinforces the link by using an idea, an image, a phrase that is commonplace or, perhaps, just plain vulgar—the comparison of how he writes, one word at a time, with the construction of the Great Wall of China: "One stone at a time, man. That's all. One stone at a time. But I've read you can see that motherfucker from space without a telescope" (x). (One can envision King holding up a hand here for a high-five.) Later still comes the signature aspect of King's communiqués to readers—the apt illustration—when he describes why he wanted to restore The Stand to its original form: "It's like a Cadillac with the chrome stripped off and the paint sanded down to dull metal. It goes somewhere, but it ain't, you know, *boss*" (xi).

Variations on these three techniques—the personal bond, the colloquialism or vulgarity, and the apt illustration—can be found in virtually all of King's missives to readers. He is particularly adept at the third, selecting points of similarity that intersect perfectly with an ordinary middle to lower-middle class milieu. In "Why I Was Bachman," for example, King confesses: "My wife accuses me of being an impossibly picky Virgo and I guess I am in some ways—I usually know at any given time how many pieces of a 500-piece puzzle I've put in, for instance" (v). He mentions in Danse Macabre that the final manuscript for The Stand weighed 12 pounds; "the same weight," he continues, "as the sort of bowling ball I favor" (399). And then there's the Big Mac and large fries quotation from Different Seasons cited above.

The sum effect of King's periodic reminders of what he shares in common with his readers is to create a club-like mentality whereby readers recognize themselves in King's ideas, beliefs, and daily activities. A final example, from Skeleton Crew, showcases the author-reader connection:

> Most thanks are to you, Constant Reader, just like always—because it all goes out to you in the end. Without you, it's a dead circuit. If any of these do it for you, take you away, get you over the boring lunch hour, the plane ride, or the hour in detention hall for throwing spitballs, that's the payback. (Introduction, 17)

Makes one feel like a vital link in the chain of King readership, especially if one fits the profile of jigsaw puzzles, autobody shops, bowling alleys, and fast food joints. If it's a pose, it's a clever one. My own belief is that, to use King's own phrase, it comes from the gut. But there are signs that King may be feeling a bit uncomfortable in this role. Consider, for example, the cryptic comment offered in the Introductory Note to Four Past Midnight:

> How good it is to know that *you* are still *there* alive and well and waiting to go to some other place—a place where, perhaps, the walls have eyes and the trees have ears and something really unpleasant is trying to find its way out of the attic and downstairs, to where the people are. That thing still interests me ... but I think these days that the people who may or may not be listening for it interest me more." ("Straight Up," xvi)

It's hard to be an ordinary Joe, after living in King's tax bracket for very long.

Giving Academia the Bird

Just as King may be feeling the squeeze of wealth and fame in relation to his fans and his fiction, his attitude toward being taken seriously by critics and scholars also shows signs of strain, despite his repeated attempts to distance himself from academia. King has understandably resented the barrage of sneers, quips, and sucker punches leveled at him from critic-scholars. The example this article began with is about par for that course. But perhaps the most damning aspect of his reception by academic readers is the fact that most have not read King, and apparently refuse to do so, either out of a stubborn refusal to acknowledge any living writer as scholarly viable (particularly if he or she is a genre writer) or out of an automatic distrust of his popular appeal. King's defenders have decried this state of affairs, but there is a sense in which King gives as good as he gets when it comes to academia. An academic scholar picking up The Stand, for instance, perhaps to see what all the commotion is about when it comes to King, will enter some pretty hostile and unflattering territory.

Glen Bateman is the resident academic in the Boulder Free Zone, but King makes it perfectly clear that Bateman is a maverick not to be lumped in with the run-of-the-mill ivory tower jarheads who people academic institutions. Nevertheless, even Bateman has to surrender the last vestiges of his academic credentials—the rationally-based principles that have heretofore governed his work in sociology—before becoming a fully accepted, fully acceptable, member of the cast of survivor-heroes. Thus, he becomes an advocate for white Magic as an antidote to the Dark Man's evil, presumably leaving all the other rationally-obsessed techno-maniacs over with Flagg to see that the trains run on time.

Bateman also gets the seal of approval because he takes a self-denigrating approach to the academic culture he represents. An entry in Fran's diary reads:

> After some persuasion Mr. Bateman has agreed to
> come along with us. He sez that after all his articles ("I

51

write them in big words so no one will really know how simpleminded they are," he sez) and boring twenty years of students to death in SY-l and SY-2, not to mention Sociology of Deviant Behavior and Rural Sociology, he has decided he can't afford to turn down this opportunity. (531)

Notice the careful juxtapositioning of Fran's misspellings and Bateman's assessment of academic pursuits. Bateman's ultimate acceptance into the post-apocalypse culture presented in Stand is signified late in the novel out in the desert when Ralph Brentner pays him a telling compliment: "I always thought those college teachers was sissies, but that man sure ain't" (1038). Again, the assessment of academia is accompanied by a grammatical error to highlight the distinction between cultures.

King no doubt scores points with the bulk of his audience in this kind of portrayal, since most readers have probably thought along similar lines at one time or another. But what is the scholar to make of it? In another instance, Bateman himself attributes an ineffectual quality to the academic activities he has devoted his life to when he, Stu, and Harold argue over what to do about Mark's appendicitis. After snapping at Harold's suggestion that they try to operate, Glen pauses:

> Harold, I apologize. I'm very upset. I know this sort of thing could happen—pardon me, *would* happen—but I guess I only knew it in an academic way. This is a lot different than sitting in the old study, blue-skying things. (539)

By and large, this attitude rules the day throughout the Free Zone: thinkers are held in suspicion if not contempt, whereas doers are very much in demand. In Stu's words, such thinkers are too often "awake at the lectern and asleep at the switch" (744).

King establishes this perspective early in The Stand, even before events transpire that make action so vital to survival. After all, had it not been for the plague Bateman might have been content going it alone, blue-skying things while the real world passed him by. In Chapter 2, King presents an even more debilitating view of the academic type in Jess Rider—"a practicing college-student-under-graduate-poet. You could tell by his immaculate blue chambray workshirt" (13). Fran, who supposedly loves Jess, can't help caricaturing him behind his back. During their argument over what to do about Fran's pregnancy, she accuses him of being "'Joe College all the way. If a mugger came at you with a knife, you'd want to convene a seminar on the spot'" (19).

A particularly revealing episode along this line of inquiry takes place shortly after Fran and Jess's argument, when Fran talks to her father about Jess. She describes a poetry reading she attended with Jess, during which she got the giggles:

> "They—the giggles, I mean—just came out of nowhere. I kept thinking, 'The scruffy man, the scruffy man, we all came to listen to the scruffy man.' It had a beat, like a song you might hear on the radio. And I got the giggles. I didn't mean to. It really didn't have anything to do with Mr. Enslin's poetry, it was pretty good, or even with the way he looked. It was the way *they* were looking at him." (57)

This is precisely the kind of giggling response King often displays toward those in academic environments who become so enraptured with the pretentions of literature that they lose track of its basic function—to communicate with readers, to tell stories. Take, for example, King's comment in Danse Macabre regarding a paragraph from Shirley Jackson's The Haunting of Hill House:

> Analysis of such a paragraph is a mean and shoddy trick, and should almost always be left to college and university professors, those lepidopterists of literature who, when they see a lovely butter-

fly, feel that they should immediately run into the
field with a net, catch it, kill it with a drop of chlo-
roform, and mount it on a white board and put it in
a glass case, where it will still be beautiful and… just
as dead as horseshit. (268)

King appears ambivalent in this stance at times, however, or even
disingenuous. Immediately following the passage cited above, he continues: "Having said that, let us analyze this paragraph a bit." He seems
to want it both ways, even if in this instance he promises not to "kill
it or mount it" (268). He ingratiates himself with readers who want no
part of such academic "lepidoptery" (and Lord knows there is no shortage of those), yet he goes on to display considerable skill in just such
an endeavor. It is a recurring habit of King's, a habit I believe has
brought him to something of a quandary in terms of his literary ambitions. But more on that later.

An Invitation to Dance

Many popular novelists lay claim to the extra-literary reader, the lay
reader, a kind of Everyreader. What distinguishes King from most of the
rest is his attempt to cultivate broad appeal while also flashing his credentials as an authentic figure in the American literary pantheon. King has acknowledged his aspirations to "build a bridge between wide popularity and
a critical acceptance." Interestingly, he also confides, "But my taste is too
low, there is a broad streak of the *vulgate*, not the 'vulgar' in my stuff. But
that is the limitations of my background, and one of my limitations as a
writer" (Goldstein, 8).

I think one might legitimately question whether King's "low taste"
is indeed a limitation. It may be the very thing that allows him to retain the essential humility necessary to so convincingly broadcast on
his readers' wave length while simultaneously exposing them to the
possibilities of fiction beyond telling a good story. King would never
deny the primacy of spinning a good yarn. But he is also well aware
of other elements that factor into the creation of successful, long-lived
works of literature. If he weren't, why would he feel it necessary to

take pot shots at other bestsellers, as in the following from *Time;* "I get angry about being compared with certain brand-name writers who sell megabillions of copies. Michener is one. I can't read him. Ludlum is another one. I was paid to review one of his books. He's the clumsiest, most awful writer. No style" (Kanfer, 80).

What standard, one might ask, does King hold his fellow commercial heavyweights to if not the very one by which he is so ignominiously pummeled on a regular basis? In instances like this King reveals that the work of practiced scholars and critics may be of more import to him than he lets on. He accuses Ludlum of no style as if it were the writer's curse of curses, yet he himself has been quoted as saying that "Style is expendable. You don't need it to tell a good story" (Underwood and Miller, *Bare Bones,* 94). Perhaps not. But if you have presumptions about the long-term literary value of your work, then of course it enters into the creative equation.

I note all this not simply to point out inconsistencies in King's opinions, but rather to illustrate that I believe King often sells himself short when he shrugs off his own literary significance and takes broad swipes at the more high-minded arbiters of so-called "taste" in American letters. It plays well in Peoria, but there's a hollowness, a falseness, to it that contrasts with the general honesty and integrity of his work. One danger inherent in adopting too hostile or too cavalier a stance toward critics and scholars is that readers, well aware of his attitude, will make a point of ignoring aspects of King's work that make it so much more than good storytelling—aspects King goes out of his way to instruct them to recognize.

That King does go out of his way to do this, even when it lays him open to attack from critical purists, makes him unique, and is one of his major contributions to contemporary fiction because it assumes an audience for literature beyond those who share a near obsessive relationship to books. What it means on a practical level is that on many occasions King will develop a paragraph, embellish a character, or incorporate an allusion with the intelligence, skill, and finesse of a master; while on other occasions a practiced reader will, to borrow a phrase from William Zinsser, "hear the laborious sound of cranking" (76). Yet, on the latter occasions I think there's often a method to King's approach, that it's not just a matter of being clumsy. The method involves meeting readers on their own turf and, without pretense, without contempt, without irony, showing them some finer points of how to read a novel.

Peter Straub, venturing into similar territory in regard to The Shining, refers to King's style in that book as "not at all a literary style, but rather the reverse. It [makes] a virtue of colloquialism and transparency" (10). I would qualify Straub's assessment with the contention that at times it is indeed a literary style; other portions of the book, however, are just as he describes. That King can pull this off is testament to the sincere identification he feels with his readers, and to the trust they invest in him.

When King's admirers mark his unique ability to bridge the popular with the academic, there's an important presumption operating beneath the surface level of their opinions: that such an ability will elevate the state of contemporary literature in general, as lay readers become aware of what the standards of academic appreciation entail. A larger body of "educated" readers, the logic goes, will demand an ever-increasing supply of Good Books.

It is an inviting scenario. The problem with it, however, is that too often those who sponsor it believe the means by which such elevation will occur are the very ones by which academic culture has set itself off from mainstream readers—an adjunct body of literary criticism. Michael Collings's defense of the Starmont series on King (of which you are holding an example) provides evidence of this belief:

> [The Starmont books] try to bridge the often too-
> apparent gap between academic criticism and gen-
> eral readership by approaching King from two direc-
> tions: first, by showing that the standards of tradi-
> tional and contemporary literary criticism might be
> justifiably and beneficially applied to King's writ-

ings; and second, by showing readers that some familiarity with those standards may be helpful in appreciating and understanding more fully King's achievements. (78-79)

Collings's point is well-taken. And if I didn't subscribe to it myself you wouldn't be reading this. Yet, despite the fact that there are already more books about Stephen King than by him, and that this trend is bound to continue and probably escalate, these books are read primarily by a small band of King fanatics (and I use that term with the most positive of intentions) or critic-scholars of contemporary fiction (inside or outside of the academy). Most of King's steady readers, his all-encompassing Constant Reader, will not seek them out, or even desire to read them. My guess is that King, too, sees lit-crit as at best an indirect path to the desired end—exposing his general readership to the standards of academic criticism. In fact, instead of relying on external others to direct readers' attention to features of higher literary ambitions, King does it himself, *within the context of the novels and stories.*

He does this in a number of ways. To lay the groundwork he first opens up the entire literary process, from publishing details to the inspiration for stories, in the front and back matter of his various books as well as his voluminous collection of other non-fiction pieces. King has without doubt spent more time than any of his contemporaries simply explaining exactly what it is he does for a living. He thus lifts the shroud of mystery or mystique that often obscures what it means, on both a practical and creative level, to be a writer. In doing so, he makes readers that much more receptive to other more arcane aspects of his work—aspects academics often piece together through repeated reading and microscopic scrutiny of his texts. King tries to save the reader such effort and keep the reading process pleasurable on its most basic level, that of story.

One of the simplest ways he accomplishes this is by reminding readers of elements that help establish motifs in the stories. In The Stand, for instance, when Larry Underwood waits to be presented to the assembled crowd at the Boulder Free Zone Open Meeting, readers are reminded three times of the Larry Underwood they met in the early part of the novel: (a) "There were five hundred and eighty people here and most of them didn't have any idea that Larry Underwood wasn't no nice guy, or that the first person Larry Underwood had attempted to take care of after the epidemic had died of a drug overdose" (753); (b) "In his heart he heard his mother's voice: *There's something left out of you, Larry*" (754); (c) "Wayne Stukey on that long ago beach saying: *There's something in you that's like bitin on tinfoil*" (754).

A practiced reader, trained to recognize character development or to go back and trace its pattern once a character has been transformed, might well sense a bludgeoning effect in this recapitulation of Larry's progress through the novel. But for someone focused exclusively on plot through most of the book, such an approach offers a moment's pause in which he or she might consider exactly how the plague and its aftermath have shaped Larry into a more humane being.

Another device King employs to expose the inner workings of his characters is a kind of point-blank explanation of their motivations. When Nadine Cross finds the planchette that will ultimately seal her fate, King introduces a psychological concept into the description of her activities: "Something had impelled her into the shop, and when she had seen the planchette in its gay party box, a terrible struggle had gone on inside her—the sort of struggle psychologists call aversion/compulsion. She had been sweating then as now, wanting two things at the same time: to hurry out of that shop without looking back, and to snatch the box, that dreadful gay box, and carry it home with her" (774).

This is a good example of what Straub calls King's transparency. A more complex, and perhaps academically satisfying, approach would be to work the pattern of aversion/compulsion more subtly into

Nadine's thoughts and behavior without calling direct attention to the concept, allowing readers well informed enough to recognize the concept for themselves. Of such recognitions are dissertations born. But King's instincts are more inclusive. He wants all readers to "get it," whether or not they have benefited from numerous years of post secondary schooling. In fact, King views his novels, to some extent, as a more entertaining substitute for such schooling.

King's most pronounced maneuvers in terms of this inclusive approach to readers are in the area of literary allusiveness. He fills readers in on the literary-historical-cultural background materials that help shape and enrich the meaning of his own works, without requiring 4 to 8 years study in college literature classes. That's not to say King isn't capable of more subtle, sophisticated varieties of allusiveness—his use of both the Bible and Milton's Paradise Lost in constructing The Stand indicate that he is. The Dark Man, whom Winter refers to as a "Miltonic superman" (67), is particularly rich in sources for King's portrayal. For analysis of these and other allusive aspects of The Stand, one need only peruse other essays in this volume.

The allusions in The Stand that serve the larger purpose of meeting readers on their own intellectual back porch offer as rich a reward for someone not specially trained in spotting such things as the most obscure reference might for a devoted scholar. And, after all, there are really two basic ways to train in such endeavors. One is to spend many years in undergraduate and graduate study, the other is simply to read, and grow into a familiarity with the richness and complexity literature can offer the interested reader. King obviously serves the latter as much as, if not more than, the former.

He offers a clue as to why this is so when explaining his method of analysis for Danse Macabre: "Although many of the books and films discussed in the pages which follow are now taught routinely in colleges, I read the books, saw the films, and formed my conclusions pretty much on my own, with no texts or scholarly papers of any type to guide my thoughts" (xv). King sees this not only as a legitimate way to arrive at an understanding of literature and culture, but a valuable way, because in one sense it is more authentic—generated from within rather than imposed from without. Although King's allusions are offered from without, they operate also as a means of placing more material at the reader's disposal to help formulate judgments, without the theoretical or methodological axes academics often have to grind.

One extended illustration from The Stand shows how King uses allusions to both enrich his tale and his readers' body of knowledge about the specific elements that go into the telling of that tale. The illustrative allusion, which amplifies the whole struggle taking place to define the post-apocalyptic society of the novel, comes from Yeats's poem "Second Coming." It first appears in the chapter where Starkey, after being relieved of his Project Blue duties, discusses with Len Creighton the impending consequences of what they have helped unleash. Notice the familiar nod to readers who may have no idea who Yeats is as King sets up the reference: "Starkey was looking at the monitors again, 'My daughter gave me a book of poems some years ago. By a man named Yeets. She said every military man should read Yeets. I think it was her idea of a joke. You ever heard of Yeets, Len?'" (175-176).

Creighton's reaction highlights the basic decency with which King approaches his readers in a case like this: "'I think so,' Creighton said, considering and rejecting the idea of telling Starkey the man's name was pronounced Yates" (176). What follows is a lengthy dialogue which is worth quoting in its entirety for what it reveals about King's method. Here's a man, Starkey, who can't get Yeats's name right, and who admittedly doesn't understand much of his poetry, but who nonetheless pointedly expounds on one of the greatest poems of the twentieth century at the precise moment it is about the best and only reference to suit the circumstances of the story, as well as King's extratextual conception of the story:

"I read every line," Starkey said, as he peered
into the eternal silence of the cafeteria. "Mostly be-

cause she thought I wouldn't. It's a mistake to become too predictable. I didn't understand much of it—I believe the man must have been crazy—but I read it. Funny poetry. Didn't always rhyme. But there was one poem in that book that I've never been able to get out of my mind. It seemed as if that man was describing everything I dedicated my life to, its hopelessness, its damned nobility. He said that things fall apart. He said the center doesn't hold. I believe he meant that things get flaky, Len. That's what I believe he meant. Yeets knew that sooner or later things get goddam flaky around the edges even if he didn't know anything else."

"Yes, sir," Creighton said quietly.

"The end of it gave me goosebumps the first time I read it, and it still does. I've got that part by heart. 'What rough beast, its hour come round at last, slouches toward Bethlehem to be born?'"

Creighton stood silent. He had nothing to say.

"The beast is on its way," Starkey said, turning around.

He was weeping and grinning. "It's on its way, and it's a good deal rougher than that fellow Yeets ever could have imagined. Things are falling apart. The job is to hold as much as we can for as long as we can." (176)

Judging this scene on a purely literary level, it is clumsy at best. There is something approaching the ludicrous in the way Starkey moves from an ignorant statement, "Didn't always rhyme," to the analytical acuity of "It seemed as if that man was describing everything I dedicated my life to, its hopelessness, its damned nobility," and then to quoting Yeats's classic line verbatim. I think King realizes this. I also think that had he wished to he could have incorporated the Yeats reference in a more sophisticated, even obscure, manner. But as it reads, you can't miss it. You simply have to make the connection between "Second Coming" and the events about to unfold in The Stand. James Twitchell, remarking on King's seamless translation of popular culture into the activity of his novels, writes that King uses "no intellectual filter, with no self-conscious art" (104), which is a good description for the process employed in quoting Yeats. Again, King wants his readers, all of his readers, to get it.

That doesn't mean King never applies a more self-conscious method to such matters. He even does so for the Yeats reference once the link to his story is so obviously established. Thus, he can perhaps satisfy those who might find the initial presentation awkward and out of place, in addition to inviting others to follow the trail of allusions now that he has lead them so deliberately to it. For example, in describing the Walkin Dude a short time after the conversation between Starkey and Creighton, King offers the following:

> *Because something was coming....* His time of transfiguration was at hand. He was going to be born for the second time, he was going to be squeezed out of the laboring cunt of some great sand-colored beast that even now lay in the throes of its contractions, its legs moving slowly as the birthblood gushed, its sun-hot eyes glaring into emptiness. (184)

Later still, Len Creighton's radio relayed message echoes the Yeats allusion as the country succumbs to panic and devastation: "'Things fall apart. The center does not hold'" (224). One could argue that such a thought might be voiced in this situation without the elaborate set-up of Starkey's conversation with Creighton, and those with the appropriate background in literary studies would surely grasp its import. But since King wants everyone to grasp its import, he risks offending the sensibilities of more highly trained readers rather than have such an important element be overlooked.

King returns to the Yeats allusion a couple more times late in the novel. The first reference accompanies Trashcan Man's dream of the Dark Man's gathering forces of evil: "Then he saw an army of ten thousand raggle-taggle castoff men and women driving east, driving across the desert and into the mountains, a rough beast of an army whose time had come round at last" (581). The second pertains to Nadine's final surrender to Flagg: "But the time had... well, it had slouched around at last, hadn't it?" (782). These are handled deftly. And for anyone paying attention, the entire series adds up to a recurring motif in The Stand, a motif King helps his readers to identify through the directness of its initial introduction into the text. The Yeats allusion is an instructive example of King's belief that "What has to come first is total accessibility to the reader" (Underwood and Miller, *Bare Bones*, 94).

Overall, the transparent, inclusive nature of King's fiction indicates that within his chest beats the collective heart of all those English teachers who tried to convince us that reading Beowulf was fun. But King tempers his proselytizing zeal with the instincts of an ad man who knows exactly what buttons to push to get his desired results. King's favorite pupils, his pets, to follow the analogy a bit further, are the millions who read him but who have never really developed a long-lasting relationship to books—the kind of relationship we automatically assume for readers of serious fiction. King's mission seems to be to foster this kind of relationship. Leslie Fiedler's description of what it means, really, to be a teacher is especially apt when it comes to King:

> The teacher, that professional amateur, teaches not so much his subject as himself. If he is a teacher of literature, he provides for those less experienced in song and story, including the reluctant, the skeptical, the uncooperative, the incompetent, a model of one in whom what seemed dead, mere print on the page, becomes living, a

way of life—palpable fulfillment, a transport into
the world of wonders. (114)

As a novelist, and a teacher of literature, Stephen King is just
such a model. He may be one of the more important teachers we
have in contemporary America, in terms of preserving that which
so often seems in its death throes—"mere print on the page." Particularly for those potential readers turning increasingly to elec-
tronic forms of communication, education, and entertainment,
King offers transport into Fiedler's world of wonders, by picking
them up at their front doors rather than waiting for them at some
suburban literary depot. Once aboard, many find it a hell of a ride.

Rock On

If we dismiss Mr. Queenan's black T-shirt crowd from our consideration and appreciation of Stephen King's accomplishments, we
risk ignoring an important element in his success. Rock music critic
Dave Marsh has described rock 'n roll as a form of "culture for the
uncultured and a means of expression for those to whom more rigor-
ously credentialed channels are denied" (ix). King's contribution to
contemporary fiction might be viewed in a similar light, with the ca-
veat that it also has much within it to recommend to the most disci-
plined of readers. Marsh goes on to say that one of his fervent beliefs
is that rock is a "self-sufficient mode of expression" and in no need
of being elevated to suit the tastes of dilettantes who find rock in its
most accessible forms beneath consideration as music "that matters."
The same can be said of King. His fiction need not be elevated to another more refined level of literary expertise in order for it to matter.
It matters now.

King characteristically downplays his own contribution to contemporary fiction by observing only that he has transformed the horror genre. He has done much more than that. For starters, he has re-
acquainted (or acquainted) a huge segment of our image-obsessed,
electronic-junky culture with the joys, both simple and complex, of
sitting down with a good book. No mean feat.

WORKS CITED

Blue, Tyson. The Unseen King. Starmont Studies in Literary Criticism No. 26. Mercer Island, WA: Starmont House, 1989.

Collings, Michael R. The Stephen King Phenomenon. Starmont Studies in Literary Criticism No. 14. San Bernardino: The Borgo Press, 1991.

Fiedler, Leslie. What Was Literature? New York: Harper & Row, 1982.

Goldstein, Bill. "King of Horror." Publishers Weekly 24 Jan. 1991: 6-9.

Herron, Don. "Horror Springs in the Fiction of Stephen King." Fear Itself: The Horror Fiction of Stephen King. Eds. Tim Underwood and Chuck Miller. New York: Signet/New American Library, 1985: 75-99.

Kanfer, Stefan. "The Novelist Sounds Off." Time 6 Oct. 1986: 80.

King, Stephen. Afterword. Different Seasons. By King. New York: Viking, 1982: 519-527. Danse Macabre. 1981. New York: Berkley Books, 1983. Introduction. Skeleton Crew. By King. New York: G.P. Putnam's Sons, 1985: 13-18. A Preface in Two Parts. The Stand: The Complete and Uncut Edition. By King. 1978. New York: Doubleday, 1990: ix-xii. The Stand: The Complete and Uncut Edition. 1978. New York: Doubleday, 1990. "Straight Up Midnight: An Introductory Note." Four Past Midnight. By King. New York: Viking, 1990: xi-xvi. "Why I Was Bachman." The Bachman Books: Four Early Novels by Stephen King. By King. New York: Plume/New American Library, 1985: v-x.

"Letters." New York Times Book Review 20 Oct. 1991: 54.

Marsh, Dave. Foreword. Fortunate Son: The Best of Dave Marsh. By
    Marsh. New York: Random House, 1985: ix-x.

Molarsky, Mona. "Back in the World." Rev. of In Country, by Bobbie
    Ann Mason. The Nation 18 Jan. 1986: 57-58.

Queenan, Joe. "And Us Without Our Spoons." Rev. of Needful
    Things, by Stephen King. New York Times Book Review 29
    Sept. 1991: 13-14.

Schweitzer, Darnel. Introduction. Discovering Stephen King. Ed.
    Darrell Schweitzer. Starmont Studies in Literary Criticism No.
    8. San Bernardino: The Borgo Press, 1986: 5-7.

Solomon, Andy. "Scared But Safe." Rev. of Four Past Midnight,
    by Stephen King. New York Times Book Review 2 Sept.
    1990: 21.

Spignesi, Stephen J. The Shape Under the Sheet: The Complete
    Stephen King Encyclopedia. Ann Arbor, MI: Popular Culture,
    Ink., 1991.

Straub, Peter. "Meeting Stevie." Fear Itself: The Horror Fiction of
    Stephen King. Eds. Tim Underwood and Chuck Miller. New
    York: Signet/New American Library, 1985: 7-13.

Tucker, Ken. "Landon and 'US.'" Entertainment Weekly 20 Sept.
    1991: 44-46.

Twitchell, James B. "Preposterous Violence in Prose Fiction: The
    Coronation of Stephen King." Preposterous Violence: Fables
    of Aggression in Modern Culture. By Twitchell. New York:
    Oxford UP, 1989: 90-128.

Underwood, Tim, and Chuck Miller, eds. Bare Bones: Conversations on Terror with Stephen King. New York: McGraw-Hill, 1988. eds. Kingdom of Fear: The World of Stephen King. New York: Plume/New American Library, 1986.

Winter, Douglas E. The Art of Darkness (Expanded and Updated). 1984. New York: Signet/New American Library, 1986.

Zinsser, William. On Writing Well: An Informal Guide to Writing Nonfiction. 4th ed. New York: Harper-Collins, 1990.

CHAPTER FOUR

The "Power of Blackness" in The Stand

Leonard Cassuto

> [T]his great power of blackness . . . derives its force from its appeals to that Calvinistic sense of Innate Depravity and Original Sin, from whose visitations, in some shape or other, no deeply thinking mind is always and wholly free.
> Herman Melville, "Hawthorne and His Mosses."

My epigraph, one of the most frequently cited passages in all of American literary criticism, was penned by Melville near the end of his work on Moby-Dick. The quotation looks forward to a generation of American literary criticism[1], but more important, it also looks back to Melville's actual subject: American literature's Puritan legacy. Though it is set firmly in the near future, Stephen King's The Stand shares this inheritance. It is an old-fashioned American romance that looks back to early New England. The Stand shares the roots of nineteenth-century American romantic fiction, and like his canonical predecessors in the genre, King roots around in the Calvinistic blackness that makes up its foundations. The Stand has a prominent historical consciousness, perhaps the most conspicuous of any Stephen King novel. King shows that he shares the dark Puritan muse of Hawthorne (the subject of the famous lines above), Poe, and Melville. I mean to examine the Puritan heritage of the book, and in the process uncover the novel's connections to the classic canon of American literature.

The Puritans' obsession with faith, correctness, and goodness resulted in a corresponding need to detail all that was apostate, incorrect and evil—so that it could be avoided. Throughout, their focus was on God's plan for New England. According to the Calvinist doctrine of predestination—to which the Puritans subscribed—God's plan was all worked out and beyond human comprehension. But predestination had myriad subtleties in interpretation that lead to different views of human possibility for good and evil. The Puritans wrote no fiction, but in the hands of their American descendants who did, these differences lead to a tension between free will and determinism. The Stand is a modern meditation on these ancient tensions, enhanced by the thoughts of early American romancers on the subject.

Evil Within and Without

Tracing the roots of The Stand begins with a look at the shifting Puritan conception of evil. Andrew Delbanco's recent book, The Puritan Ordeal, tracks the changing Puritan views of evil and sin, a back and forth movement from an emphasis on privation (lack of grace) to the opposite view relying on an outside agent (Satan). The former position centers on what Delbanco calls "a significant absence" (25), causing a lassitude that keeps one from reaching for what is good. Doctrinally speaking, evil lies inside all of people as original sin, a necessary ingredient of the human condition. The tragedy of this sin for the Puritans, says Delbanco, is one of incompleteness; it separates the petitioner from God. Anne Bradstreet writes in "To My Dear Children" that "it is the absence and presence of God that makes heaven or hell" (Puritans 140).

The second view places evil on the outside, as a malevolent agent (Satan) who seeks to establish dominion over the world by conquering weak humans: the people, in turn, have to band together to resist Satan's thrall—with the necessary divine support. Puritan preachers could (and did) point to the external agency of evil to explain any external misfortune from Indian attack to witchcraft. The representation of evil as an outside force implies that it be a nearly irresistible one. The warning here is that the devil will catch all who stray from the covenant (represented by the polity), and he will annex the souls of all who let down their guard.[2]

The possibility of resistance implies human input into the outcome, which would appear to violate the spirit of predestination. But the doctrine allows for this possibility of free choice. Despite the emphasis on an immutable divine plan, there remains a place in predestination for human free will, with a crucial catch: people want to do what God wants them to do. Through this early brand of doublethink, the Puritans could call for the exercise of willful self-discipline even while they counseled that God has designated the elect for all time, regardless of whether one summons this discipline or not. For the Puritans, says Perry Miller, God's reasons "had to be guessed or, as often as not, foregone" (NE Mind: The Seventeenth Century, 16).

The Stand encompasses both the inside and outside views of evil. In representing both together, King places them into debate. He thereby sets up an opposition whose implications reach down to the foundations of Puritan theology. In the process, he also manages to set up a related argument on predestination. Each view of evil has two major paradigms in all but one are characters who become simultaneously archetypal and real.[3]

The two primary examples of external evil in the novel are the plague and the figure of Randall Flagg. The uncut includes more material on the origins of the plague than the original version does, but this added information fails to part the veil of secrecy that surrounds covert government activity in the novel. Despite the new details of how the flu bug got out, the essential human motive is still missing. King lets us see lots of activity of lower-level operatives, but he makes sure that we never find out the big the one that would explain what makes people do these things. Deep motive is shielded from us; in its place we see people following orders. In short, government remains an inscrutable agent of evil, and for all the detail, the disease itself is still fundamentally a mystery throughout.[4]

In The Stand, government is not of the people or by the people (not regular folks, anyway), and it's certainly not for them. Given this lack of connection, it's important that the major characters in The Stand who survive the plague are all social outsiders in one way or another.

This plot device increases the inscrutability of the government, which becomes an external, shadowy, malevolent entity—like the dark man himself. In secular terms, the social contract is violated long before the plague occurs. Viewed from the religious perspective that underlay the original Puritan theocracy in New England, the covenant between man and God (symbolized in part by the state) has been broken. Only after the plague can government and covenant be re instituted together, ushered in by a spiritual rendition of "The Star Spangled Banner."

Randall Flagg is the other major outside agent of evil in The Stand, a spirit in nominally human form (though with no palm lines). Though Flagg is clearly allied in some way with Satan, King leaves the nature of the connection ambiguous. (Nick suggests that he is "the scared, bad part of all of us" [503]— which would put him into the "inside" category of evil—but Mother Abagail vigorously disagrees, later calling him "the Devil's Imp" [648]. The hypnotized Tom Cullen uses traditional associations to suggest that Flagg is the devil himself [807, 1110].) Flagg blends human and supernatural attributes. At first he needs human credentials. Once he acquires an identity, his otherness becomes more and more pronounced as he uses his powers, which include levitation, an (almost) all-seeing eye, magical transformations of self and objects, and mystical, telepathic influence over people and animals (especially wolves, weasels, and other wild beasts of the night). Though Flagg shows signs of human weakness (a hot temper, for example), it is clear that he is not human, and that he possesses physical powers that can physically overwhelm our kind.

The Stand initially appears to rely on this outer manifestation of sin and evil, but it draws heavily on the inside view as well. The Puritan view of evil as coming from inside the self holds that it is inherent to the human condition, a tendency that can (and indeed, must) be resisted by faith in God, manifested through participation in God's community (in this case New England). In this view, evil—or sin—becomes a personal act of choice, an act of free will (though according to Calvinist predestination, this free will is exercised in conjunction with God's plan).

The clearest examples of chosen (or internal) evil are Harold Lauder and—in a murkier way—Nadine Cross. These characters question the extent of their control over their own lives, and wind up fighting for it. In the end, they choose their own way. By virtue of such storylines, The Stand serves as a kind of casebook of evil archetypes: it's all-inclusive.

Harold Lauder is a thinking human being who nourishes his own dark side for self-centered (rather than community-based) reasons. Harold is an eccentric but basically goodhearted soul when Frannie comes upon him in Maine. As a lonely teenager who suffers from a lack of attention, he seizes upon the chance to make a friend of Frannie, who is (it seems at first) the last person on earth with him. Harold's gradual moral declension results from his failure to merge his desires with the community; it takes place when, in Hawthorne's words, "his heart cease[s] to partake of the universal throb" (375).

Harold turns to Flagg, but King has Harold emphasize more than once that he does so of his own free will. Harold has several clearly defined moments of choice. The first of these comes when he decides to read Frannie's diary (561). The second is in his room in Boulder, "when faced with the knowledge that he was free to *accept what was*, [he] had rejected the new opportunity" (672). Finally, there is his Faustian bargain with Nadine (794-5).

Nadine's case is more complicated, since the lure is much stronger for her; her ouija board experience (769-770) shows that Flagg has selected her far in advance. But even under these circumstances Nadine retains her own will. Her view of herself blends active choice and passive submission in a curiously conflicted way: "She wanted to go to him . . . but she didn't want to. He was meant for her, but he terrified her. . . . She began to feel like the prize ring in a tug-of-war rope" (628). Later, she feels that "all the choices have been taken away" (763). The narrator describes her soon afterwards as "beyond help or hope of succor" (771). For her own part, she calls her bargain with Harold "the thing I have to do" (794). When she goes into a trance and wakes up in a drive-in, she realizes that "Flagg had driven her as a man might drive a car or a truck" (861).

From this it would seem that Nadine has no choice, or any free will at all, for that matter. But if this is so, then what is it in her that continues to resist? Why does she go to see Larry in the hope of sleeping with him to break the spell? The child prophet Joe/Leo Rockway says that Nadine acts "on purpose." And indeed she does. Even after Flagg rapes her and the "iron gates" of insanity close behind her (975), she manages that not only to recover her sanity momentarily, but also to use that instant to bring about her own death (and that of Flagg's unborn child) by goading him into killing her. She dies with a "great smile of relief and triumph on her face" (1002), with the joy borne of freedom of choice.

This opposition between evil within and evil without has implications for human capacity in general—and especially for human culpability. For if the evil agent simply overpowers the hapless human, then where is the sin? If one is doomed from the start, then where is one's own moral agency? On the other hand, if evil is simply an internal matter and a question of personal choice, then how do we explain Flagg's powerful thrall? The Stand never clears up this conflict. Instead, King sets up an enduring tension between chance and determinism, between free choice and fate. The characters argue about where evil comes from and how to fight it, but there is no resolution.

The enduring question in the novel surrounds Flagg's power over the human will, and by extension, his power to determine events. Can Flagg overwhelm human faith? Can he force a person to serve him against that person's own wishes? The answer is curiously and compellingly ambiguous, and it becomes the fulcrum of the debate about the nature of evil in the book. When Dayna Jurgens is being interrogated by Flagg, she realizes that she must kill herself because she is otherwise powerless to resist him. On the other hand, when Glen Bateman laughs in Flagg's face from a prison cell not long afterwards, Flagg appears impotent, and can only order Lloyd to kill his captive.

Flagg appears to require human weakness. When he liberates Lloyd from prison to serve him, he seems to require Lloyd's assent to the Faustian bargain before his plan can proceed. He offers speech to Nick Andros in a dream, but Nick rejects the deal, and Flagg can't use him after that (361).

Flagg's power to determine events is similarly inconsistent, with the flaws frequently tied to the imperfections in his roving eye. He plans Harold Lauder's fatal accident perfectly, but when Harold almost shoots Nadine afterwards, it comes as a surprise to him. When Trashcan Man interrupts Flagg's planned execution of the Boulder delegation with a nuclear bomb, the intrusion exposes another blind spot: "He had foreseen everything but this" (1068). Why is Flagg able to control only some of the people for only some of the time? His spotty powers become the basis for the debate over human self-determination in the face of evil in The Stand.

The story of Harold Lauder is the other side of the question of human capacity. In Puritan terms, Harold is an example of how temptation by evil leads one to violate the ideal nature of man. The sin is Harold's own, and the presence of Flagg is less relevant to it than his betrayal of his friends. Or is it? Significantly, each one of Harold's key moments of choice is tinged with ambiguity. When he gives in to the lure of the diary, the narrator tells us that "maybe it was already too late" for him to turn back (561). In his room, he is conscious that "The malignancy drew him" (672). And when he agrees to conspire with Nadine, the narrator tells us that he "succumbed to his destiny" (795). Does Harold choose his own fate, or is he the "little windup toy with the key sticking out of its back" (967) that Flagg believes he is? Harold is sure of his own independence—and that counts for something. When he sets off his bomb, he does so with the words, "I do this of my own free will" (876). And in his dying statement he reemphasizes this fact (964). But the narrator is less certain—and so, perhaps, is the reader.

This debate boils down to a tension between the early and later Puritan conceptions of evil, an opposition which King links to the question of free will. The difference is between evil without (with its implications of determinism) or within (which implies free choice). The Stand reenacts the recurring conflict between them. The Puritans never stopped the pendulum from moving between the two, and neither does Stephen King. In Mother Abagail's terms, the question is whether people are "the potter or the potter's clay" (902). She is clearly on the side of the clay, but she also adds that "There's always a choice. . . . Your will's still free" (905). Such double-talk doesn't exactly solve the problem, but it is typical of discussions of predestination.

King updates this old argument in The Stand, showing its affinities to the new one between nature and nurture, which we see in some of its popular modern versions—the book touches on alcoholism and the insanity defense, for example. The question centers on moral responsibility for action. Are people free agents or not? The last word here should be Harold Lauder's, for more than any other human character, Harold becomes the focal point of this debate. Harold concludes that "Your GOD, Your DEVIL, owns the keys to the lighthouse; I have grappled with that so long and hard in these last two months; but to each of us he has given the responsibility of NAVIGATION" (856). This enigmatic comment strikes an ambiguous balance that is followed throughout the book.

The addition to the novel of the concluding scene with Flagg extends this test of predestination to the depiction of time, and thus makes it all the more equivocal. An anonymous Boulder resident says before the stand that they're all living out the book of Revelation (888). (The "holy fire" at the end (a modern apocalypse) is good evidence to support this.) This statement describes millennial time, a linear progression to the last judgment. But at the book's end, Flagg is there again, making not a line but a circle, an endless cycle. Is time a circle or a line? Like most of the conflicts that I've been discussing so far, this one is ancient. The Puritans, like other biblical thinkers of their own time and before, believed in the line (or, as Stephen Jay Gould calls it, "the arrow"[5]) and repressed the cycle. King deliberately leaves the question open.

Indeed, The Stand leaves all such fundamental questions hanging. The novel stands as a challenging but intellectually faithful exploration of Puritan ideology. King is questioning our intellectual roots and embracing their contradictions.

Narration and Predestination

This questioning takes place in the narration of The Stand as well as the content of the plot. Moby-Dick is told by a symbolically named outsider, Ishmael, who has no special window into the mind of Ahab, and even less insight into the inscrutable whale. The reader filters all information and judgment of fate, free will, prophecy and predestination through its various unreliable—and often conflicting—sources. The Stand has a different angle of approach to these issues because it is told by an omniscient third person narrator who frequently reminds us that he knows the outcome of it all, even if we readers do not. This technique allows for an unusual variation on predestination in the narration itself.

If, as in the Calvinist scheme of things, God is the ultimate author who knows the story because He made it up, then the narrator of The Stand must have God's ear, because he also knows what's going to happen. Ordinarily, this kind of narrative omniscience would be a truism, but King makes it into an issue by turning the narrative presence into a coy dropper of hints, sly clues, and even a red herring.

This is not a matter of direct foreshadowing (of which contains plenty), but of simple narrative intervention. For example, the narrator informs us that Nick and Tom aren't exactly free of Julie Lawry (414) when she isn't due to reappear for some 500 pages. Likewise, we are told that Trashcan Man's final conflagration (also hundreds of pages further on) will be "very great" (617). These hints get more pointed and frequent as the book goes on. Kojak the dog, the narrator tells us, will outlive Glen Bateman by sixteen years—so we can start preparing for the sociologist's death long before it happens (737). These offhand comments can be straightforward—as when we are told that Dayna's spy mission will result in no one seeing her again in

Boulder (833)—but they can also be frustratingly enigmatic, as when the narrator comments that Larry would later remember the judge's quip about suicide "in bitter circumstances"[6] (799).

This is narrative omniscience of a peculiar, self-conscious kind. The narrator tells us what's coming, but in a tricky way, so that we don't know what to expect. When Stu breaks his leg on the way to Las Vegas, the others leave him and the narrator remarks that "they never saw Stu Redman again" (1042). The reader has every reason to assume that the injured Stu is doomed, but of course this is not the case; it is the others who die. Have faith in me, the narrator seems to be saying. If you jump to conclusions, you'll lose track of the story. The result of this trickery is a kind of Calvinism in the narrative itself. The reader has to have faith in the author of the grand plan. This is a structural return to the content of the plot: form merges with content.

The narrator's showy omniscience contrasts sharply with the storytelling limitations of the characters in the story. The differences make The Stand into a kind of contest in storytelling. Mother Abagail, Flagg, and the prophets (Leo, Tom Cullen) compete as story tellers, shapers, and makers. (Various other characters are granted moments of foresight, and these also shape the story. For example, Frannie foresees Harold's bomb and saves most of the committee as a result.) Events separate the true and false prophets. Events also expose the their limitations. Mother Abagail is one of the most powerful presences in the book, but her prophetic ability has explicit boundaries ("Would he win? That was not for her to know. . ." [643]). Even more pointed is her admission on her deathbed that she is "not allowed to know" (902, emphasis added). Mother Abagail is a good storyteller (her visions certainly affect events), but she is not the equal to the teller of the tale, a narrator with God's ear.

Neither is Flagg, whose narrative orchestrations contain small but crucial flaws. Nadine wonders "Just how much control over events did Flagg have?" (840). Mother Abagail's answer echoes Milton's scheme in Paradise Lost: "[A]ll things serve the Lord. Don't you think this black man serves Him too? He does, no matter how mysterious His purpose may be. The black man will follow you no matter where you run, because he serves the purpose of God, and God wants you to treat with him" (504). Perhaps Mother Abagail is correct here. The dark man can direct certain movements, but the storyteller conducts the whole opera. The only one who appears to know as much as the storyteller is the retarded Tom Cullen. When Tom goes under hypnosis, he knows all—but at those times he's "God's Tom," the most farseeing prophet in the book. Tom is actually prepared to give the whole story away at one point, but Ralph stops him (807). Because Tom doesn't reveal the outcome and no one else can, the result of this storytelling competition in The Stand is the enforcement of divine—and hence narrative—authority. When the story is predestined, only the author knows all.[7]

The Puritans and the American Renaissance

Exploring this linked series of curious oppositions (time, free will) has been an enduring preoccupation of our national literature. As a dialogue on the nature and source of evil, falls into the historical line of American romancers, our literary lovers of ambiguity. The dark fiction of the American Renaissance frankly acknowledges its Puritan legacy, and like The Stand, it distills questions from it, not answers. Poe's, Melville's, and Hawthorne's shared preoccupation with evil found different expressions in their fiction. The ideas of all three together inform The Stand, much more than they do King's other novels, thereby making the book into a thematic throwback to our most famous literary tradition.

King explicitly acknowledges his American Renaissance forbears in the novel, backing up a collection of shared themes with a series of inter-textual references. These references are not accidental, nor are they gratuitous shows of learning. The clearest proof of their importance comes from examination of Harold's death scene. As Harold lies on a edge of a cliff preparing to pen his farewell to "the world who never wrote to me" (724, an earlier reference to Emily Dickinson, whose loneliness and isolation give some meaning to Harold's own).

79

At this point, the narrator tells us that "he had never stopped his long-hand entirely, remembering that Moby-Dick had been written in long-hand, and The Scarlet Letter, and Paradise Lost" (959). Why these books? Because they contain some of the most famous writing ever done on the major themes (free will and determinism, guilt and duty, the deathless battles of good and evil, love and death) which are at the center of The Stand. Second, consider: Milton was blind when he composed Paradise Lost, so he never put pen to paper himself. King wants that book in the list, even if it doesn't exactly belong there. Such references are not just homages; they bear directly on the what The Stand is about. Because The Stand treats themes visited most often by Poe, Hawthorne, and Melville, it is worth examining the ways that King refers to, draws from, and builds on their work.

Like Poe, King focuses in. The Stand on those who, like Harold Lauder, have chosen to oppose others instead of joining them. Poe's isolatos invariably share this quality, with similarly unfortunate consequences. Virtually all of the inter-textual glances toward Poe in The Stand come while the focus is on Harold.[8] Harold's situation calls forth Poe references because he is tortured in the same kinds of ways. In fact, Harold would fit quite well into certain Poe tales. Like William Wilson, he rejects his conscience. Like "The Black Cat" narrator, who tortures and kills his pet precisely because it loves him, Harold chooses pride and hate because he convinces himself that they are "more noble" than love and community. For both Harold and Poe's narrators, these decisions lead to murder. Though King tells us more about Harold than Poe's readers usually learn about his tortured narrators, secrecy is not an issue here. Like Montresor in "The Cask of Amontillado," Harold simply chooses to be alone.

Hawthorne's characters share this tendency to isolation, but Hawthorne focuses on the guilt that accompanies it rather than the psychosis that results. King carries this theme faithfully into The Stand. All of the main characters struggle with guilt that comes from a sense of duty; how to cope with it is a major theme in the book.[9] Larry Underwood is unquestionably the Dimmesdale character of The Stand, but unlike Dimmesdale, Larry gets a chance to redeem himself for his pre-plague self-absorption. His character moves from self-centered to social, finally sacrificing himself for the others. Nadine, the original object of his affections, moves the other way, from community to self. She and Harold are the Ethan Brand figures of The Stand, guilty of the unpardonable sin of isolation.

The Las Vegas characters, most notably Barry Dorgan and Paul Burlson, have no sense of guilt—and this is mainly what separates them from their Boulder counterparts. Dorgan, for example, joins Flagg out of a policeman's desire for order, but he won't acknowledge the moral implications of his choice. These characters refuse to think about what they've done, and that makes them culpable, no matter how neutral their decision to join may have been. It is more than coincidental, I think, that the nuclear holocaust that climaxes the book results from Trashcan Man's guilt and his desperate search for redemption (1007). Like Hawthorne, King wants to highlight the need for mutual connection, and the duty that arises from it.

King shares a great deal of Puritan ground with Melville in The Stand. Like Melville's Ahab, The Stand asks questions about human will and its role in shaping experience. Moby-Dick and both explore the tension between free will and fate. Ahab's drive to know the unknowable is conducted against the tide of numerous prophecies, beginning with Mad Elijah's warning, and continuing through the Parsee's three Macbeth-like predictions. Ahab claims total freedom of action, mastery over even the fire he worships: "I own thy speechless, placeless power; but to the last gasp of my earthquake life will dispute its unconditional, unintegral mastery in me" (119, 417).[10] Even so, Ahab seems very much in the grip of something bigger than himself:

What is it, what nameless, inscrutable, un-

earthly thing is it, what cozening, hidden lord and
master, and cruel, remorseless emperor commands
me; that against all natural lovings and longings, I so
keep pushing, and crowding, and jamming myself on
all the time; recklessly making me ready to do what
in my own proper, natural heart, I durst not so much
as dare? (132, 444-445)

Moby-Dick offers no final answer. Ahab comes off as a figure of towering free will, but all of the prophecies that lead Ishmael
to call his ship "the fated Pequod" (125, 426) turn out to be true.
The book comes full circle, ending where it begins, with a lone
orphan.

The Stand also grasps its own tail in this way. Flagg's final
scene with the natives (added to the revised version) reminds him
that "Life was such a wheel that no man could stand on it for long"
(1141). Like Moby-Dick, The Stand questions whether we are the
potter or the potter's clay. Like Melville, King offers no answer:
the last words of the originally released version of the novel are
the simple "I don't know" (817).

In tracing these themes to their ultimate non-resolution, The
Stand follows a belletristic trail back to the Puritan question of
where evil comes from: in the heart or outside it. This question
started it all, and it has remained an American preoccupation. King
covers this venerable national path in a traditional vehicle, an
American romance.

City on a Hill

Perhaps the most American part of The Stand is its setting.
Why is this book set in America in the first place? Granted, the
plague was an American invention, but why should the stand between good and evil take place only in America? Considering that
American government officials manage to spread the plague to the
rest of the world before it carries them off, there are amazingly few
references to what is happening in other countries. Though there

are presumably survivors everywhere, we never hear of them. We can assume that they are not having dreams of Mother Abagail and Flagg, or else they would try to find a way to Boulder or Las Vegas, and some would trickle in. But are they not having dreams? We can only assume that they are exempted from the grand scheme that is being played out in America. Why should America be the site of this archetypal conflict between good and evil? Why does King not give his "tale of dark Christianity" (xv) more overtly biblical overtones by having the two cities be Jerusalem and, say, Cairo? What makes America so special? Put simply, why are we the chosen people?[11]

The setting of The Stand presents a modern version of the oldest case for American exceptionalism. This idea has flourished since Puritan times, of course (as a reading of any Presidential foreign policy speech will attest), but like most of the major themes of The Stand, the roots of American specialness in the novel extend far back into the Puritan past.

In setting the book in America, King follows the plan laid out in John Winthrop's "A Model of Christian Charity." Winthrop's famous evocation of America as "a city on a hill" has become a recurring real-life national rhetorical trope, and that trope gains literal realization in The Stand.[12] It isn't just that Boulder really is a city on a hill, while Las Vegas lies in a valley. Like New England, which Winthrop says will be watched by the world, Boulder becomes God's paradigm in The Stand — exemplary of either success or failure. King follows Winthrop in guaranteeing nothing: "if we shall deal falsely with our God in this work we have undertaken, and so cause him to withdraw his present help from us, we shall be made a story and a by-word through the world" (Puritans, 91). The Boulder natives, like those of Winthrop's New England, are not necessarily more virtuous than their counterparts elsewhere (Winthrop's sermon is frequently misinterpreted this way), but they are more accountable by virtue of their highly visible position. The Puritans saw America as special even before they settled it, a new Israel whose residents would have to live up to its promise. The same holds true for Boulder: its citizens are drawn there for a sacred aim, a task that they must perform if they are to justify the promise of their dreams.

Conclusion

In The Stand, this Puritan-inspired holy purpose merges with the secular ideals of its later incarnation, the republic of the United States. In both New England and Boulder, government is necessary for the people to achieve their goal of triumphing over evil. The people of Boulder update the ideals of Puritan theocracy, but their aim is really the same: to unite in battle against the forces of darkness. The Puritans found this darkness within and without—wherever they decided to look for it, really. The citizens of Boulder have an opponent with concrete existence, but in their case too the battle front is both inside and outside.

The Puritans created the first version of America, but their nation slowly but inexorably slid toward the secular ideals that their founders abhorred. These secular ideals became the basis for the a second creation of America, this time through revolution. The Boulder people in The Stand bring the religious ideals of Puritan New England together with the secular ones of the American revolution. They recreate "Little America" (636), a secular, democratic state with a high moral/religious purpose. By conflating two historical moments, King thus fuses Puritan concerns to modern ideals of democracy.

This all-inclusive historical vision of America in The Stand complements the novel's comprehensive approach to Puritan ideas of evil arid their foundations in predestination. The Stand is a casebook of national archetypes, from the founding of the nation to the nuclear threat. It is also a modern commentary on the most enduring moral themes in our national literature. A look back across religious, intellectual, and literary history, it is a new version of an old book in many more ways than one.

NOTES

1. For example, Harry Levin called his 1957 study of Poe, Hawthorne, and Melville The Power of Blackness. This kind of literary criticism is still being written at a good clip, as American romanticism is traced to the very tips of its roots. Recent examples include Jeffrey Steele (The Representation of the Self in the American Renaissance, 1987), Leon Chan (The Romantic Foundations of the American Renaissance, 1987), and David Leverenz (Manhood and the American Renaissance, 1989), among others. The focus may change, but "the power of blackness" remains the same.

2. Perry Miller connects the growing prevalence of this idea of evil lurking without to the gradual decline of piety in New England. He suggests that evil comes to be located outside because the people were no longer inclined to seek it inside of themselves. The clergy, wanting to jump-start the engines of personal faith, pointed ever more fervently to external misfortune (whether tangible or not) as evidence of the growing reprobate population (See The New England Mind: From Colony to Province, 179 ff.).

   Like Miller, Delbanco links the view of evil within the self to a general ideological equanimity in the Puritan community, but Delbanco's position is not so chronologically absolute. He sees the Puritans as shifting back and forth in their conception of evil, from the inside to the outside view.

3. For an in-depth discussion of this archetypal realism, see Ed Casebeer's article (Chapter 8).

4. Depicting government as the covert outside agent of evil is a consistent theme in King's work, as Tony Magistrale has shown. See "Crumbling Castles of Sand: The Social Landscape of Stephen King's Gothic Vision," 50-53. Besides The Stand,

Magistrale also cites the nefarious government activities in
Firestarter and The Dead Zone.

5. See Time's Arrow, Time's Cycle: Myth and Metaphor in the
Discovery of Geological Time, in which Gould explores the relevance
of this dichotomy to landmark discoveries in science.

6. King has inserted this prescient commentary in his fiction before, but not so frequently or as cagily as in The Stand, and not—as I
will argue—with nearly the thematic resonance.

7. King has been experimenting in recent years with authorship
as plot and theme of his books (see Misery, The Dark Half, and the
recent novella Secret Window, Secret Garden). Here, perhaps, is a kind
of precursor to these efforts, a demonstration of the limitless power of
narrative authority.

8. The references are to "The Cask of Amontillado" (675, 961
(the latter when Harold unwittingly echoes the captive Fortunato)),
"The Murders in the Rue Morgue" (725), "The Purloined Letter"
(726), "The Tell Tale Heart" (824), and "The Raven" (824).
   The sole Poe reference unrelated to Harold is the Judge's hotel room encounter with Flagg in the shape of a crow, which makes
him think of "The Raven" (921).

9. We learn at the very beginning of the book of Stu Redman's
guilt over his dead brother (4-5, and later of Frannie Goldsmith's
guilt feelings about her parents (e.g. 163, 237)). (King also has
Frannie describe herself with a reference to The Scarlet Letter
(12).) Nick Andros is not exactly guilt-ridden, but he does feel a
strong sense of duty to Tom Cullen, stemming from his memories
of his own mentor, Rudy Sparkman.

10. Citations from Moby-Dick will be given by chapter and page number.

11. Plague references in the narrative include India (164), Mexico and Chile (166), London (197), and Peru and Senegal (339). Post plague references, which tend to be conversational, are to Australia (691), India (718), Brazil (1013), and (after The Stand) Peru (1133). In each of these latter cases the speaker appears to assume that things will be different in these remote countries than it was in America.

Flagg himself wonders near the end whether "There might be another like him in Russia or China or Iran, but that was a problem for ten years from now" (999). And finally there is Flagg's final appearance on some unidentified continent, an implicit support for the American exceptionalist idea (America first, and only then somewhere else).

12. For example, Ronald Reagan framed his presidency with the image of the city on a hill, using it first in his debate with Jimmy Carter in 1980, and finally in his last state of the union address. (It is also worth noting that he used it incorrectly, to suggest national prosperity.)

WORKS CITED

Delbanco, Andrew. The Puritan Ordeal. Cambridge, Mass. and London, England: Harvard University Press, 1989.

Hawthorne, Nathaniel. "Ethan Brand," in Selected Tales and Sketches. Third Edition. New York: Holt, Rinehart, and Winston, 1950: 361-378.

Heimert, Alan, and Andrew Delbanco, eds. The Puritans in America. Cambridge, Mass. and London, England: Harvard University Press, 1985.

King, Stephen. The Stand. New York: Signet NAL, 1978, 1980. The Stand: The Complete and Uncut Edition. New York: Signet NAL, 1990.

Magistrale, Tony. "Crumbling Castles of Sand: The Social Landscape of Stephen King's Gothic Vision." Journal of Popular Literature (1985): 45-59.

Melville, Herman. Moby-Dick; or, The Whale. Norton Critical Edition, ed. Harrison Hayford and Hershel Parker. New York and London: W.W. Norton & Company, 1967.

Miller, Perry. The New England Mind: From Colony to Province. Cambridge, Mass.: Harvard University Press, 1953. The New England Mind: The Seventeenth Century. Cambridge, Mass.: Harvard University Press, 1939.

Poe, Edgar Allan. Complete Tales and Poems. New York: Vintage, 1975.

CHAPTER FIVE

Repaying Service with Pain: The Role of God in The Stand

Leonard Mustazza

In March of 1984, Stephen King described to Douglas Winter the influence that organized religion has had upon his life and art:

> Part of me will always be that Methodist kid who was told that you were not saved by work alone, and that hellfire was very long... When you are six or seven years old, that kind of stuff bends your mind a little. So it keeps coming back in my fiction. And the major reason, I think, is that I still believe that most of the ideas expressed by Christianity—particularly the progression from the Old Testament ideas to the New Testament ideas—are morally valid.
>
> My religious feelings have not changed very much over the years—they are as traditional as the stuff that I write. They are not complete. I believe in God; I believe what I write when I say that I think we live in the center of a mystery. Believing that there is just life, and that's the end of it, seems to me as primitive as believing that the entire universe revolves around the earth. (Winter, 15-16)

Generally, Methodism's central doctrine of "sanctification as the inherent righteousness of the justified who have the power to resist evil" (The New Catholic Encyclopedia, vol. 9:736) is subtly presented in many of King's works. More specifically, when he deals with religion directly, he is often critical of the excesses or abuses associated with misdirected religious observance. In this regard, one thinks of Carrie, where misguided fundamentalism is the cause of catastrophe;

of The Talisman, where corrupt evangelism is placed at the service of evil; of Salem's Lot, where the weak faith of a priest leads to his abandonment by the God he purports to serve. In each of these cases, human error, corruption, or moral frailty proves to be the source and/or sustainer of evil, and, in these instances, God as a player in the human drama is either absent altogether or given a peripheral role at best. Owing both to King's religious convictions and his artistic integrity, the notion of a *Deus ex machina*, a God who directly intervenes to settle human problems, is not a common feature in his fiction, nor does he blame God for the evil that people do. As King himself has stated, evil in fiction derives from two sources: the predestinate and the freely willed, the latter being "the sort we have no right laying off on God the Father" (Dance Macabre, 62). In other words, evil (whether supernatural or humanly contrived) exists, weak people cannot resist it, and it is up to good people to stop it. That is King's typical modus operandi.

The only notable exception to this rule occurs in one of King's longest and most beloved novels, The Stand, which Tony Magistrale has correctly called "King's most religious book to date" (Magistrale, 37). Although, as we shall see, much of the novel revolved around questions of human choice, God plays a far greater and more direct role here than He does in any other King work. Speaking of predestinate or outside evil, King asserts that the classic fictional manifestation of this concept occurs in "the Old Testament story of Job, who becomes the human Astroturf in a kind of spiritual Superbowl between God and Satan" (Danse Macabre, 62). A similar confrontation between the Old Testament God and the forces of supernatural evil is engages in The Stand, thus making the Bible a convenient intellectual framework in which to place King's view of God in the novel. Most of the time, King's religious themes revolved around the use and abuse of Christianity as a corruption or empowering system of belief. Father Callahan in Salem's Lot, for instance, fails to recognize the saving power of Christian love and selflessness, whereas Ben Mears and Mark Petrie remember and use these desirable human qualities.

By contrast, the flawed but virtuous characters in The Stand, though they must actively choose and believe in the power of the Good, are also themselves chosen to be God's champions, much as God chooses unlikely heroes in the Old Testament. Abagail Freemantle explains this idea to Nick Andros shortly after their meeting: "Nick, all things serve the Lord . . . The black man will follow you no matter where you run, because he serves the purpose of God, and God wants you to treat with him. It don't do no good to run from the will of the Lord God of Hosts. A man or woman who tries that only ends up in the belly of the beast." And when Nick asserts his atheism, Mother Abagail simply laughs and says, "Bless you, Nick, but that don't matter. *He* believes in *you*" (515-16). The God of The Stand is not the merciful God of the New Testament, but the unyielding God of Job and Moses, ad it is in this context that I would like to consider the divine presence in the novel.

That The Stand at its inception was predicated in part upon religious principles is suggested by King himself when he describes how the idea he came to him. At work on an abortive fiction concerning the Patty Hearst kidnapping, King one day heard a "Bible-thumping" radio preacher utter a phrase that would soon change his artistic plans: "Once in every generation the plague will fall among them." King was so taken with the phrase that he wrote it down and tacked it over his typewriter. At about the same time, he read about a chemical-biological weaponry accident in Utah that, had the wind not blown in the opposite direction, threatened the populace of Salt Lake City. The incident reminded him of a sci-fi novel, George R. Stewart's Earth Abides, in which a survivor of a plague on earth witnesses the ecological changes wrought by the end of humankind (Danse Macabre, 398-99; see also Winter, 55). Before long, King abandoned his plans for the Patty Hearst novel, and slowly, painfully, The Stand was written instead. The accident in Utah, a conspiracy of human error and the human desire to apply its technology to destructive ends, is obviously woven into the novel; so is the sci-fi notion of selective immunity to the "plague." Even the unfinished Patty Hearst novel enters The Stand insofar as the idea for a "dark man with no face" was suggested by the news photos of SLA member Donald DeFreeze. However, the most intricate and intriguing part of the mix concerns King's fascination with the Biblical phrase used by the radio preacher, for, ultimately, the influence of the Bible will be far greater than those of the Utah news story or Stewart's novel or the Biblical phrase taken by itself. Once King has completed the painstaking process of assembling the Boulder community, the Providential design of the fiction becomes clear.

The precise nature of that design is a matter of much critical contention. The original paperback issue of the novel in 1980 carried beneath the title the words "a novel of ultimate horror." The publisher was obviously trying with these misleading works to capitalize on King's growing reputation as a writer in the horror genre, even though few people who have commented on the book would agree with that generic tag. Criticizing Meyer Levin's review of the book, which Levin calls "a pseudo-sf/fantasy duel between God and the Devil," Charles L. Grant argues that The Stand, along with many of King's other novels, represent a contest between the universal forces of White and Dark and that God and Satan are merely small manifestations of "a far larger and more pervasive whole." Assigning the novel's characters to "these two simplistic roles ignores the broader canvas upon which King is working" (Grant, 166-67). Likewise, Tony Magistrale urges that the book represent an elaborate allegory embracing the ultimate conflict between the forces of good and evil in the world, though Magistrale adds that the conflict "is eventually defined . . . in human terms" (Magistrale, 37). Douglas Winter, also noting that King's fiction "offers not theological polemic," admits that the intervention of God in a few of King's novels provides for "a potential—and indeed persuasive—explanation of events." The portrayal of God here, Winter goes on, "hearkens less to modern Christian values and their source, the New Testament, than to those of the Old Testament, and particularly the Book of Job" (Winter, 93).

More specifically, some commentators have place the novel within conventional literary frames. James Egan regards it as "apocalyptic," albeit a secular version of that type, insofar as it represent a vision of the end of the world as we know it, accords with Northrop Frye's definition of the apocalyptic as an unveiling of the realms of heaven and hell, and "partakes of a complex dualism because it is an intellectual dialectic held together by a tension of opposites" ("Apocalypticism," 214-15). Chelsea Quinn Yarbro writes that King uses a post-catastrophic landscape as the setting for "a final confrontation of good and evil." "Beginning as a survival novel," she goes on, "it quickly shifts into gear for a proper Armageddon, complete with a very diabolical symbol of evil going to and fro in the earth and walking up and down in it" (Yarbro, 66). Deborah Notkin sees the second part of the book as "a Tolkienesque battle between good and evil" (Notkin 156), and Joseph Reino regards these apocalyptic elements as both conventionally Christian and "akin to the mythic imagery of Richard Wagner's Gotterdammerung ('Twilight of the Gods') in the nineteenth century, or the 'Ragnarok' ('Judgement of the Gods') of the Elder and Younger Eddas of medieval Nordic literature" (Reino, 51, 55). Even King himself had commented in conventional terms about the novel's theme, regarding the two camps into which the good and evil assemble as, respectively, Apollonian and "violently Dionysian" (Danse Macabre, 401).

All of these appraisals are, to some extent, valid, but most of them are also flawed, I thing, notably in their insistence that the novel is conventionally "apocalyptic" and that King is working almost entirely with a secular framework. The only definition of the tern "apocalyptic" that applies here is Frye's concept of "revealing" or "unveiling." The term itself derives from the Greek *apokalyptein*, which means "to disclose" or to "uncover," and, in this regard, what is disclosed are the supernatural underpinnings of the heretofore rationally defined universe. By the same token, a major player in the dramatic contest is God, and there can be no question that one of King's characters in The Stand is God the Father, who as he often does in the Old Testament, chooses unlikely champions, communicates with only a few, and ultimately uses his own prodigious supernatural force to dispose of his enemies. There is no end of the world in The Stand, nor is there a single Job figure who stands by while God and the Adversary slug it out. For that matter, the novel is much more akin to the Noah story than to either Job or Revelation since it involves a divine re-creation rather than a singular moral victory or a "final confrontation." Indeed, Mother Abagail herself makes this point when, in considering the superflu and why "God had brought down such a harsh judgment on the human race," she remembers that God "had done it once with water, and sometime further along, He would do it with fire" (481).

Be that as it may, it makes much more sense, I think, to apply to a specific text or theme, but rather a character, as it were-namely, the God of the Old Testament. In his many Biblical skirmishes with evil, how does God do battle? What types of people does he choose to do his bidding? What weapons does he give them, and what guarantees of personal safety does he issue to these champions? What balance finally is struck between the divine will for human action and the continued working of human schemes, good or bad? Let us begin with the most obvious and least likely of God's heroes in The Stand, a very old woman.

Abagail Freemantle has been characterized by a variety of terms, including "deity and compassionate judge . . . oracle and god" (Yarbro, 67), "Earth mother" (Winter, 58), and "mystic" (Egan, "Sacral Parody, 131). Although I doubt that King intended her to be anything like a god herself, the other terms are true enough, but also somewhat narrow in their focus. The fact is that King has gone considerably out of his way to make Mother Abagail a Mosaic figure, not in surface detail, but in function and experience. When God chooses Moses to lead the Israelites out of their Egyptian captivity, he offer no explanation as to why he has chosen Moses of all people, just as no explanation is ever rendered for divine decisions. When Moses asks "But who am I . . . that I should go to Pharaoh, and that I should bring the Israelites out of Egypt," God answers, "I am with you" (Exodus 3:11-12); when Moses again protests that he has "never been a man of ready speech" and that even now he is "slow and hesitant of speech," God responds in much the same manner he does when Job asks why he has been sent such terrible suffering: "Who is it that gives man speech? Who makes him dumb or deaf? Who makes him clear-sighted or blind? It is not I, the Lord?" (Exodus 4:10-12). God had chosen Abagail Freemantle, too, and owing to her familiarity with the Bible, the main difference between this frail old woman and the tongue-tied Moses lies in her knowing better than to protest:

> Her place was not to judge God, although she wished He hadn't seen fit to set the cup before her lips that He had. But when it came to matter of *judgment*, she was satisfied with the answer God had given Moses from the burning bush when Moses had seen fit to question. Who are *you*? Moses asks, and God comes back from the bush just as pert as you like: I *Am*, Who I *AM*. In other words, Moses, stop beatin around this here bush and get you old ass in gear. (481)

Mother Abagail's faith in God here and in many of her discourses with the others in the Boulder camp is complete, but it is not the keynote of this descriptive passage or most of her other assertions concerning God. Rather, the theme here and elsewhere has to do with divine inscrutability, irresistible selection, and fear of being chosen. Although her Christian beliefs play a role in her accepting so readily to the divine will, she knows that her own will plays almost no role in her carrying out the divine plan, any more than Moses' protests and refusals lead to his being let off the hook.

That realization concerning God's irresistible selection of his champions leads, curiously enough, to may frightened, even bitter, reflections on her part. Acknowledging the unprecedented state of disaster in the world, she realized that "now her time was coming to be a part of it and she hated it." But then she also realized that she has no alternative, for "when you questioned God, the answer you got was

I *Am*, Who I *AM*, and that was the end. When His own Son prayed that the cup be taken from His lips, God never even answered . . . and she wasn't up to that snuff, no how, no way" (482). Likewise, she later explains to Nick Andros her ambivalence toward God and the impossibility of refusing his call:

> "Oh, Nick," Mother Abagail said, "I have harbored hate of the Lord in my heart. Every man or woman who loves Him, they hate Him too, because He's a hard God, a jealous God, He Is, what He *Is*, and in this world He's apt to repay service with pain while those who do evil ride over the roads in Cadillac cars. Even the joy of serving Him is a bitter joy. I do His will, but the human part of me has cursed Him in my heart. 'Abby,' the Lord says to me, 'there's work for you far up ahead. So I'll let you live and live, until your flesh is bitter on your bones. I'll let you see all your children die ahead of you and still you'll walk the earth. I'll let you see our daddy's lan taken away piece by piece. And in the end, your reward will be to go away with strangers from all the things you love best and you'll die in a strange land with the work not yet finished. That's My will, Abby,' says He, and 'Yes, Lord,' says I, 'Thy will be done,' and in my heart I curse Him and ask, 'Why, why, why?' and then only answer I get is Where were you when I made the world?'"
> (521-22)

Based solely upon this vague (though familiar) rhetorical question, she suppresses fear and anger and prepares to wait and suffer, citing as her precedents the Children of Israel and Job, who also waited and suffered until God was ready to liberate then. She is also prepared to die, citing as her precedent here an even more impressive Biblical figure: "... it had pleased Him to allow His only Son to be hung up on a tree with a bad joke written over His head" (654). Can she reasonably expect any better treatment now that God has chosen her as his agent?

Like the world described in the various books of the Old Testament, the world in which Mother Abagail must carry out the divine will is rotten to the core. Selfishness, gratuitous aggression, and dishonest, at both the personal and official levels, are common and accepted features of life on earth, notably in the Untied States—the nation responsible for inventing the superflu as a weapon of mass destruction. The social and political climate of the novel intentionally mirrored the malaise that King felt in the nation. At the time of the book's composition, America suffered from a variety of seemingly insoluble ills—economically motivated gas shortages, runaway inflation, the resignation of the President, our ignominious loss in Southeast Asia, raging debates over the right to life as opposed to the right to choose. So frustrated was King with these and personal troubles that he admitted to taking a perverse glee in "doing a fast, happy tap-dance on the grave of the whole world" in The Stand (Danse Macabre, 400). Within this greater sociological and artistic context, Mother Abagail's simple faith in God and ready acceptance of the bitter task at hand become all the more remarkable and admirable. Moreover, this context also enlarges the scope of the fictional struggle. In contrast to the cosmological proportions of the great moral struggle between God and his Adversary through human agency, failed or corrupt human designs involving politics or economics or technology seem to be little more than selfish and futile games. If, as Mother Abagail believes, we are the *children* of God the *Father*, then our contrived systems are akin to the sometimes elaborate games that children play to the amusement of their wiser parents—games that are tolerated when they lead to simple diversion, encouraged when they result in moral instruction (e.g. a sense of fair play), and stopped when they turn violent, petty, or selfish. The last of these is clearly the case in The Stand, which as I indicated earlier, has much

97

in common with the Biblical story of Noah. Just as God becomes "grieved at heart" over the violence and other evils of humankind there (Genesis 6:5-14), so the God of King's novel decides to start this world over again as well.

As noted above, it is Mother Abagail herself who subtly recalls the Noah story by alluding to the connection between God's judgmental destruction of the earth by water long ago and the current global catastrophe (481). Curiously, however, it is also she who, for all her serious theological intentions, sees the events unfolding here as a kind of game, with God taking the role of the ultimate "gamesman." "If He had been a mortal," she thinks, "He would have been at home junkering over a checkerboard on the porch of Pop Mann's general store back in Hemingford Home. He played red to black, white to black. She thought that for Him, the game was more than worth the candle, the game *was* the candle. He would prevail in His own good time" (654). Later, Nick Andros says much the same thing, that "we are all part of a chess game between God and Satan" (707).

As Mother Abagail knows, however, the price of being a chess piece in this moral contest between the ultimate gamesmen is pain. "He's apt to repay service with pain," she tells Nick (521), and that is a bitter lesson she has learned from he beloved Bible. The examples found throughout the Old Testament are myriad: Abraham's test of fidelity though his willingness to sacrifice his son Isaac (Genesis 22:1-18); the blind Samson perishing along with his enemies, the Philistines (Judges 13-16); Saul losing his status as divinely protected king because of a breach in religious decorum in presenting the whole-offering himself rather than waiting for Samuel (1 Samuel 13:9-14); and, of course, Job's horrible testing in what amounts to a bet between God and the Adversary. In the cases of Samson and Saul and others (e.g. Solomon, whose worship of foreign gods prompts God to withdraw his favor [1 Kings 11:1-13]), it is true that willed disobedience leads to their abandonment by God, though one might still wonder whether their previous faithfulness does not warrant a second chance. The case

98

that is most troubling is that of Moses, who is not allowed to see the Promised Land after many years of service because he takes credit for a divine miracle (Numbers 20:1-13). Moses' "sin" is one that God will not tolerate ever since it was first perpetrated by Adam and Eve, the sin of *pride*, placing one's own desire for self-aggrandizement before glory of God. Mother Abagail had always feared this error, which she calls "the mother of sin," and, when she eventually falls prey to pride, to enjoying the attention that she receives from the others and thereby taking the place of God, she goes into the desert " to find my place in His work again," as she writes in her leave-taking note. "I will be with you again soon if it God's will" (720). She will return briefly to charge God's heroes, but, like Moses, her "sin" was great enough in God's sight to deny her the chance to see the completion of God's work. Like Moses, she dies before she can see the Promised Land, in this case, America Restore, if only tenuously.

The task of defeating the formidable Randall Flagg now falls to the other "heroes" whom Gad has assembled in the Boulder camp, all of them as unlikely as many of the heroes of the Old Testament. The naive Joseph who turn his Egyptian captivity into a boon to himself and his family, the scheming Jacob who becomes the great patriarch Israel, the diminutive David who becomes one of the greatest kings from among the Israelite tribes—all of theses and others are reflected in the secular (and, for the most part atheistic) champions of The Stand. Randall Flagg delights in the prospect of confronting these men, fully believing that the likes of the laconic Stu Redman, the self-indulgent Larry Underwood, the egghead sociologist Glen Bateman, the deaf-mute Nick Andros, and the simpleton Tom Cullen can match him. And it's true—none of them, left to his own devices, would stand a chance against Flagg's powerful magic or his technological might.

The point is, however, that they are not left to their own devices, any more than is Moses, who, when asks how he can take on a pow-erful ruler like Paraoh, is told simply, "I am with you" (Exodus 3:12). The question that such divine guidance raises, however, is very sig-nificant: it, to use Mother Abagail's metaphor, these characters are "chess pieces" being manipulated by God "the Gamesman," where does the characters' own volition—free will, in other words—figure in the scheme? The issue of free will in King's work is a thorny one, indeed, though many critics have tended to overlook the thorns. Deborah Notkin, for instance, argues that "to defect from good to evil is a simple act of will; to leave evil for good is at best extremely dangerous and at worst literally impossible" (Notkin, 156). While this statement is applicable in certain limited instances in King's work (e.g. the courageous choice made by the frightened adult protagonists in It) ironically, there is not, by any stretch, a consistent philosophy concerning the efficacy of volition in King's work. Does Louis Creed in Pet Sematary choose the evil that overtakes his life? Is his goodness as a friend, a father, a husband, a physician enough to protect him? How much choice does Jack Torrance have in The Shining to cling to whatever humanity and love he has left after the Overlook begins its evil work? Indeed, given their guiding dreams and Mother Abagail's foreknowledge of their arrival in Boulder and their ultimate roles in the conflict, how free are the protagonists of this novel?

Ironically, the agent who have the greatest capacity for free will seem to be those whose morality is questionable to begin with, an idea that occurs elsewhere in King's fiction, too. A prime example is Father Donald Callahan in Salem's Lot. Once a man of strong faith and unwavering conviction in the potency of his church and his God, Father Callahan has come to doubt that potency, and, as a result, he cannot call to his aid the power of God to defeat Barlow in their direct confrontation. By contrast, Ben Mear's simple faith in the power of goodness (though not necessarily in God) allows him to turn a cruciform object made of medical tongue depressors into a very powerful tool. Even more impressive and effacious are the faith and innocence of a little boy, Mark Petrie, whom even the formidable Barlow comes to fear and respect. "The boy makes ten of you, false priest," Barlow tells Callahan (Salem's Lot, 355), just before he "feeds" the priest his own perverse "communion."

Likewise, in The Stand, those who are marginally good to

begin with have the free will to resist evil, notable Harold Lauder and Nadine Cross. These characters, Tony Magistrale correctly maintains, "succumb to Flagg's machinations because they lack the self-discipline to exert a moral will" (Magistrale, 21). Similarly, Bernadette Lynn Bosky, writes that "Harold makes ongoing choices: the possibility of turning away from evil is present at each step, although each denial makes choosing the good more difficult the next time" (Bosky, 264). Even Winter, who believes that Harold's "choice for evil is less than a free one," admits that his moment of recognition just before he dies "suggests that this choice in never irrevocable" (Winter, 60). In fact, even as they choose to do evil, both Nadine and Harold express a great deal of doubt about their choices, particularly at the moment of their deaths. "He had fallen victim to his own protracted adolescence," Harold admits to himself. "He had been poisoned by his own lethal visions." And, then, in his final written communication, he publicly asserts his culpability: "I apologize for the destructive things I have done, but do not deny that I did them of my own free will" (978). In a moment of fleeting sanity, Nadine Cross, too, exercises her will to thwart Flagg's grand designs, forcing him to kill her himself. Although she does not articulate as much as Harold does in his dying gesture, King's description of what Flagg sees in her face when he kills her show her tactfully doing much the same thing. As the furious Flagg hurls her through the window, "he saw the great smile of relief and triumph on her face, the sudden sanity in her eyes, and understood" (1016).

By contrast, in direct opposition to Winter's position that evil characters are somehow less free than their morally superior counterparts, I would argue that, while there are strong predispositions to goodness in Stu, Larry, Glen, and the others, choice in itself is not the key motivating factor in their proceeding with the task of reinventing America and, more important, battling supernatural evil, anymore that Moses can choose to lead the Israelites or Job can choose the suffering that is thrust upon him. In some sense, King's discussion of "predestine evil" in Danse Macabre can be tailored to the situation here and called "predestined good," a concept that is seen throughout the Old Testament. After her mystic experience in the wilderness, Mother Abagail herself makes this point abundantly clear to her fellow agents in God's name:

> "Electric lights ain't the answer, Stu Redman. CB radio ain't it, either, Ralph Brentner. Sociology won't end it, Glen Bateman. And you doin' penance for a life that's long since a closed book won't stop it from coming, Larry Underwood ... You propose nothing in the sight of God."
>
> She looked at each of them in turn. "God will dispose as He sees fit. You are not the potter but the potter's clay. Mayhap the man in the west is the wheel on which you will be broken. I am not allowed to know."
>
> "God didn't bring you folks together to make a committee or a community," she said. "He brought you here only to send you further on a quest ... you must lead, Stuart. And if it's His will to take Stu, then you must lead, Larry. And if He takes you, it falls to Ralph."
>
> "Looks like I'm, riding drag," Glen began. "What—"
>
> "Lead?" Fran asked coldly. "*Lead*? Lead where?"
>
> "Why west, little girl," Mother Abagail said. "West. You're not to go. Only these four." (917)

In this scene, one of the most emotionally charged of the novel, Mother Abagail makes clear that choice or volition are not factors in the quest westward; the same God who chose her to lead, gave her the physical and emotional strength to assemble the chessboard army, and punished her for her pride, will manipulate this final confrontation, too. When Frannie hysterically protests against Mother's harsh theology,

Mother is granted the power to provide a sign of God's might. Like Moses performing miracles in the sight if Paraoh, like David's slaying Goliath, like Jesus performing wonders in the name of his Father, Mother Abagail seized Frannie's wrist and cures the whiplash she suffered in the explosion that killed Nick. This gesture of divine potency puts to rest not only Frannie's hysteria but also any doubt about the nature of the mission they are to undertake. Even Frannie's feeble protest that her cure is God's "bribe" and that she'd rather have the pain back so that Stu might be spared (918) suggests that she now believes in that God's potency, too. And when Larry asks if there is a choice and Mother answers in the affirmative (920), the characters' (and the readers') belief in completely free will is severely undermined by what they have just witnessed. And so, she orders them westward to make their "stand": "You will go, and not falter, because you will have the Everlasting Arm of the Lord God of Hosts to lean on. Yes. With God's help you will stand" (919).

That "stand" begins with their westward trip on foot through the desert, a trying journey that has as much to do with internal renovation as battle strategy. By the time the group, minus the injured Stu, reaches Las Vegas, they are more than prepared to do the divine will, even to martyr themselves for a moral cause. Like Tom Cullen, who describes himself as "God's Tom" in his hypnotic trance earlier (819), they, too, become God's agents, and their status as such is measured by the moral and intellectual changes they have undergone prior to this critical point in the narrative. Two characters in particular stand out in this regard.

By the time he is imprisoned by Flagg's forces, Glen Bateman, the most articulate and emotionally detached of the entire Boulder community, has abandoned the rationalist philosophy he earlier espoused and end by echoing Mother Abagail's metaphysical words: "I am not the potter, nor the potter's wheel, but the potter's clay; is not the value of the shape attained as dependent upon the intrinsic worth of the clay as upon the wheel and the Master's skill?" (1069). Tony Magistrale has argued that these words "tersely represent King's religious orientation as it appears throughout the canon . . . If a divine Being does indeed coexist with humankind in animation King's world, Its influence is 'dependent upon the intrinsic worth' of the men and women who gave shape to Its destiny" (Magistrale, 38). I would agree, but I would also point out that the ultimate determiner of such a worth in the Bible and this Biblically inspired novel is God, not other people and often not the characters themselves, who often express surprise over their "election." So it is that Bateman can echo Mother Abagail's words about individual life as clay and God as the potter; so it is, too, that he can face his greatest fear—confronting Flagg directly—and laugh. Finally, that laughter will cost Glen Bateman his life at Lloyd Henreid's hands, but not before his intellectual and emotional immersion in divine philosophy (in sharp contrast to his earlier sociological rationalism) becomes complete. In the end, following a far higher authority than Mother Abagail, Glen echoes the words of the dying Jesus when he tells his murderer, "It's all right, Mr. Henreid . . . You don't know any better" (1072). Like the broken Christ forgiving his enemies before commending his spirit into his Father's hands, Glen Bateman finished his divine work of further thwarting Flagg's diabolical plans and, perhaps more important, further eroding Flagg's beliefs in his own invincibility.

Larry Underwood, the other hero divinely directed to take a "stand" against evil, is even more impressive with regard to the changes he undergoes in the novel. Through the first third of the novel, there is a continual doubt raised—by his friends, his lovers, his mother, even Larry himself—about his motives for action. The suggestion in all of these doubts is that Larry is essentially a selfish person. Douglas Winter, noting that Larry's character stands in marked contrast to the more traditionally heroic Stu Redman, writes that Larry "is self-destructive and avoids taking responsibility until it is thrust upon him. But in the final trumps, his refusal to give up the good inside himself transforms him into a person capable of self-sacrifice" (Winter, 59). I agree that his essential goodness is evident throughout the novel, and, therefore, his decision ultimately to lay down his life for his friends comes as no real surprise. However, the heroic Larry of the end of the novel is not simply an evolved form and the one we meet at the beginning, as is pretty much the case with Stu Redman, who changes very little over the course of time and harsh experience. Larry changes continually. He chastised himself when he fails to take care of Rita Blakemoor; he refuses Nadine's advances, despite his desire for her, because he remembers his commitment to Lucy Swann; he takes his political role in the Boulder community seriously as he does his charge by Mother Abagail, though she cannot assure him or any of the other men that he will survive in the end; when Stu falls and cannot continue the journey, it is Larry who expresses the greatest sympathy, even sorrow, for his friend, who he believes will surely die in the wilderness. Perhaps more than any other character in this or any other King novel, Larry Underwood embodies a central tenet of Methodism, with which King was indoctrinated as a child. "Methodism's doctrine of Christian perfection emphasizes not the possibility of sinlessness, but rather perfection in love and motives" (New Catholic Encyclopedia vol. 9:7739). Larry's character evolves until such "perfection in love and motives" becomes perfectly evident. In fact, given this evolution, one might even consider him finally a greater hero than Stu. It falls to Larry to become the gallows moralist, telling the assembled Las Vegas community of Flagg's evil and their own fear and cowardice, and it also falls to Larry to name God as the final disposer of this conflict, recognizing as he does the "Hand of God," the holy fire that would consume righteous and the unrighteous. And his response to this divine intervention is not all what the earlier and more selfish Larry might have said: "'Oh God, thank God', Larry thought. 'I will fear no evil'" (1085). Although he dies along with the "unrighteous," Larry Underwood can thank God for choosing him, for counting him among the most righteous.

Not unexpectedly, commentary on the meaning of the end of The Stand is divided. Egan ("Apocalypticism," 221) and Winter (65) see Frannie and Stu and Adam and Eve figures going off on their own to forge a kind of Eden in Maine. Reino regards Peter, the son born to Frannie, as representing "a somewhat imperfect yet obviously intentional analogy with the Christ child," a claim base primarily upon the child's being the son of "Jesus," whose name recalls that of Jesse, the father of David, from whose line Christ descends (Reino, 63). King himself is far less sanguine about the end of this book, seeing the surviving principals as neither Adam and Eve emparadised nor the potent youthful Jesus. "... I came to realize that the survivors would be very likely to take up all the old quarrels and then all the old weapons," King has said. "Worse, all those deadly toys would be available to them ... My own lesson in writing The Stand was that cutting the Gordian Knot simply destroys the riddle instead of solving it, and the book's last line is an admission that the riddle still remains" (Danse Macabre, 402-03). When King wrote these words, the last line of the novel is spoken by Frannie, and it concerns whether people have learned anything from this terrible experience. "I don't know," is the conclusion she reaches. The uncut version of the novel published in 1990, however, ends on a far different and more ominous note. Here, we see a resurrected Flagg (named Russell Faraday) among primitive natives in a jungle, preparing to make them "civilized." He will give them the tools of civilization, notably technology, thus allowing the "wheel" of life eventually to come "round to the same place again" (1153). That this "wheel" continually turns, culturally and morally, is all too true, but from a Biblical perspective—the proper context for this novel, I believe—the turning wheel also brings cyclical confrontation between the traditional powers of divine good and infernal evil, and in each of these skirmishes, the good is reasserted, tenuously maintained, and finally lost, only to bring the wheel full circle again. This is the theme of The Stand, to show this cycle of good and evil and to celebrate the good, which the God of the Old Testament and the New continually allows to grow out of earthly corruption and supernatural influence. By the same token, however, "good isn't free," as King maintains (quoted in Winter, 81), and neither is service to God. Divine service is repaid with pain; death comes to the righteous along with the unrighteous. But goodness—moral glory in this exegetical fiction—in this world is not possible without such pain, and that is a lesson learned from Methodist pulpits and from life itself, that King has incorporated into his artistic universe.

WORKS CITED

Bosky, Bernadette Lynn. "The Mind's a Monkey: Character and Psychology in Stephen King's Recent Fiction." In Kingdom of Fear: The World of Stephen King. Ed. Tim Underwood and Chuch Miller. 1986; rpt. New York: Signet 1977: 241-76.

Egan, James. "Apocalypticism in the Fiction of Stephen King." Extrapolation 25 (Fall 1984): 214-27.

Egan James. "Sacral Parody in the Fiction of Stephen King." Journal of Popluar Culture 23 (Winter 1989): 125-41.

Grant, Charles L. "The Grey Arena." In Fear Itself: The Horror Fiction of Stephen King. Ed. Tim Underwood and Chuck Miller, 1982; rpt. New York: Signet, 1985: 165-71.

King, Stephen. Danse Macabre. 1981; rpt. New York: Berkley, 1983. Salem's Lot. 1975; rpt. Signet, 1976. The Stand. The Complete and Uncut Edition. NewYork: Doubleday, 1990.

Magistrale, Tony. Landscape of Fear: Stephen King's American Gothic. Bowling Green, OH: The Popluar Press, 1988.

"Methodism." In The New Catholic Encyclopedia. 17 vols. New York: McGraw-Hill, 1967-79: vol 9:735-41.

The New English Bible with Apocrypha. Oxford Study Edition. New York: Oxford University Press, 1976.

Notkin, Deborah L. "Stephen King: Horror and Humanity for Our Time." In Fear Itself: The Horror Fiction of Stephen King. Ed. Tim Underwood and Chuck Miller, 1982; rpt. New York: Signet, 1985: 151-62.

Reino, Joseph. Stephen King: The First Decade, Carrie to Pet Sematary, Boston: Twayne, 1988.

Winter, Douglas E. Stephen King: The Art of Darkness. New York: New American Library, 1986.

Yarbo, Chelsea Quinn. "Cinderella's Reveng—Twists on Fairy Tales and Mythical Themes in the Work of Stephen King." In Fear Itself: The Horror of Stephen King. Ed. Tim Underwood and Chuck Miller, 1982; rpt.. New York: Signet, 1985: 61-71.

CHAPTER SIX

Free Will and Sexual Choice in The Stand

Tony Magistrale

In Danse Macabre, Stephen King's nonfictional analysis of contemporary gothic film and literature, a study which reveals as much
about King's own canon as it does about the larger genre with which
he is most often affiliated, we learn that The Stand was conceived out
of a bifurcated vision: "In the case of The Stand this meant beginning
with the glum premise that the human race carries a kind of germ
within it . . . The book also tries to celebrate brighter aspects of our
lives: simple human courage, friendship, and love in a world which
is so often loveless" (374-5). This statement embodies the moral po-
larities dramatized throughout King's fiction. The potential for King's
characters to produce acts of good or evil is always dependent upon
the individual's ability to control his or her most selfish impulses.
Those characters who are unable or unwilling to rise above "the germ"
of original sin come to embody the most destructive human tendencies. On the other hand, those who do manage to behave in a responsible manner, to embrace "simple human courage, friendship, and
love," are open to the possibilities of happiness and salvation. In The
Stand, more than any other King novel, free will and moral choice are
solidly within the individual's purview; all of the major characters in
this book participate directly in determining their fates. As Carroll
Terrell points out in his discussion of the religious implications in The
Stand, "This confirmation of the power of light over the power of
darkness allows for free will as Harold Lauder, the bright boy of the
book, understands. He may go with the light or the dark, but whatever he does, he agrees with Jean Paul Sartre, that he is condemned
to be free" (146). And late in the novel, Harold himself recognizes the
full burden of free will in one of his ledger entries: "To follow one's
star is to concede the power of some greater Force, some Providence;

yet is it still not possible that the act of following itself is the taproot of even greater Power? Your GOD, your DEVIL, owns the keys to the lighthouse; . . . but to each of us he has given the responsibility of NAVIGATION" (856).

All through the novel we witness illustrations highlighting this "responsibility of navigation" in individualized contexts. Mother Abagail supplies a plan of action that suggests Glen, Stu, Ralph and Larry engage in direct confrontation against Flagg's empire, but it is up to each individual man to choose whether or not to trust that plan and head west. When Larry asks, "'Do we have a choice?'," Abagail's response is that "'There's always a choice. That's God's way, always will be. Your will is still free. Do as you will'" (905).

The shape free will takes in this book directs the narrative itself: characters are tempted by Flagg's promise of power and pleasure and join him in the west, or choose to align themselves with the Mother Abagail's Free Zone society at Boulder. And while this decision is never an easy one to make—the novel's most complicated and engaging characters are pulled in both directions simultaneously—the decision becomes, nonetheless, a barometer for measuring the individual's moral will.

When we first encounter Glen Bateman early in the novel, he is reprimanding his dog, Kojak, availing him with instruction on behavior that is notable for its relevance to both the canine and human worlds: "'Always remember, Kojak, that control is what separates the higher orders from the lower. Control!'" (327). Bateman's seemingly innocuous remark turns out to be one of the novel's guiding principles. In his role as King's spokesman throughout the text, generally reflecting the writer's social perspective and philosophy, Bateman is also an astute observer of human history and psychology. He knows that Flagg's dominion emphasizes the wrong kind of control—tyranny rather than moral responsibility. The decisions which face the members of the Free Zone are harsh ones, but they are still highly personal choices, and the citizens are free enough to make them; in Flagg's empire, there are no choices, only duties and obedience. Bateman believes, as does King himself, that the human world is involved in a deathless struggle to distinguish our basest impulses from the most noble. If we are each free to elect our own destiny, then it is also our responsibility to behave in a manner that demonstrates control over bestial urges. The superflu has not only depopulated the globe, it has also placed those few remaining survivors into a moral vacuum; in the absence of official law and institutions, the very concept of "civilization" needs to be redefined. Without an existing system to enforce restraint, individuals feel free to indulge behavior that might have been socially objectionable in pre-plague America. We learn, for instance, that the inhabitants of the Free Zone live together without the need for matrimony, that others get drunk and walk up and down the street smashing windows of vacant homes. But the darkest implications of this breakdown in traditional social mores are most fully articulated by Stu Redman, the Free Zone's first sheriff, who realizes the inherent dangers which exist in a society without the benefit of police and judicial courts to enforce law and order. More specifically, Stu recognizes that under the current conditions of anarchy and survivalism the greatest risks are posed to the weakest members of society—children, the handicapped, and women:

> "Because the police and courts are gone and you're a woman and you're pretty and some people . . . some men . . . might not . . . be gentlemen. That's why."
> His blush was so red now it was almost purple.
> He's talking about rape, she thought. *Rape.* But how could anyone want to rape me, *I'm pregnant.* But no one knew that, not even Harold. And even if you spoke up, said to the intended rapist: "Will you please not do that because I'm pregnant," could you reasonably expect the rapist to reply, "Jeez, lady, I'm sorry, I'll go rape some other goil?" (321-2)

Throughout The Stand, the success with which an individual is capable of adhering to Glen Bateman's principle of self-control signifies which side of the Rockies that character will call home. And this is especially true when this standard is applied to sexual choices and behavior. In The Stand, particularly in the case of the 1990 revised and uncut version of the book, a character's sexual responsiveness is a way of signalling his or her place on the moral continuum of good and evil. In the realm of the Free Zone, we see evidence of healthy sexual unions; most of Boulder's men and women do not use sex as a form of manipulation or degradation. Perhaps the best examples of such relationships are between Frannie and Stu and Larry and Lucy. The latter couple is particularly important as an illustration of the manner in which King views a healthy sexual relationship as a kind of insulation against the powers of evil. When Nadine Cross tempts Larry with the offer of her virginity, it is not an offer inspired by love or genuine affection; if she ever felt such emotions for Larry, Nadine has had ample opportunities to act upon them. She comes to him now because she wishes to use him, to erect a barrier against Flagg's design to make her his dark bride. She pursues Underwood out of desperation and selfishness. And it is thus significant that her seduction is interpreted by Larry as a kind of rape, since, like a rapist, Nadine is far more interested in power than she is in sex:

> "*No!*" she said fiercely. "Let me finish. I want to
> stay here, can't you understand that? And if we're with
> each other, I'll be able to. You're my last chance....
> Make love to me and that will be the end of it. I'll be
> safe. Safe. I'll be safe..."
> A low moan came from her.
> "Larry, if you knew—"
> "Well, I don't. Why don't you try telling me instead
> of... of raping me?"
> "Rape!" she repeated, laughing shrilly. "Oh, that's
> funny! Oh, what you said! Me! Rape *you*! Oh, Larry!"
> (758-9)

In his refusal to succumb to her demands, Larry shows a level of self-control and loyalty (to Lucy) that has long been missing from his personality. The scene highlights a moral "crossroad" for both Cross and Underwood. From the point of this rejection to the end of the novel, Larry's personal ethics are never again in doubt. He has passed through the dark night of the soul, and can now lay claim to Lucy—who is pregnant with his child—as his reward. Nadine, on the other hand, views her rebuff as destiny; unlike Larry, who finally discovers the capacity for exerting his moral will, she surrenders her's to the dark man. As she walks away from Larry, her corruption is symbolically ordained in King's description of the landscape with which she merges: "She was a black shape distinguishable from other black shapes only when she crossed the street. Then she disappeared altogether against the black background of the mountains" (759).

Stephen King's women suggest a strong medieval influence; in his male-centered universe, the majority of his women characters are either madonnas or ambassadors from hell.[1] King himself appears cognizant of this dichotomy. When the interviewer from Playboy, citing critic Chelsea Quinn Yarbro, posited in 1983 that King has a problem creating "believable women characters between the ages of 17 and 60," King's response was honest and nervously apologetic: "Yes, unfortunately, I think it is probably justifiable criticism . . . I recognize the problems but can't yet rectify them" (Underwood-Miller, 47). Although the splitting of women into angels or demons is not particular to contemporary culture (every male author from the Bible to Melville's Pierre seems to conform to this paradigm), the single-dimensionality of King's female portraits is paralleled in his orientation toward sexuality. Without the blessing bond of love, sex in King's world is always lascivious and malefic, as we see embodied in sadomasochistic perversions of Trashcan Man and The Kid: "Whining, Trashcan began to stroke him again. His whines became little gasps of pain as the barrel of the .45 worked its way into him, rotating, gouging, tearing. And could it be that this was exciting him? It was. . . . 'Like it, dontcha?' The Kid panted. 'I knew you would, you

113

bag of pus. You like having it up your ass, dontcha? Say yes, or right to hell you go'" (587-8). Sex without love, be it homosexual or heterosexual, in Stephen King's fiction is always a manipulative, enticing force that pushes characters toward greater levels of depravity. And for that matter, most of the positive sexual relationships in King are between white, heterosexual couples who practice intercourse in the missionary position exclusively. Any sexual response that deviates from this norm risks at least King's quiet censorship and at worst his quasi-Biblical condemnation. In the Playboy interview, King was remarkably candid on the subject of sex, acknowledging his own personal conservatism which, in turn, translates into his fiction: "There's a range of sexual variations that turn me on, but I'm afraid they're all boringly unkinky" (Underwood-Miller, 45). As perverse sexual relations become more frequent and more intense in each of King's books, the affiliation with evil becomes correspondingly stronger. The sexual lives of the characters involved supply the reader with a visual manifestation of their spiritual corruption. Consider, for example, Tod Bowden in Apt Pupil, whose evolution of a pathological sexuality reflects his deepening involvement with a Nazi war criminal.

Since a healthy sexual response should be an affirmation of life and love between human beings, the perversion of that bond serves as an effective vehicle for portraying the loss of one's humanity, a surrendering of free will to the ravages of sin. When sex is utilized for manipulation, its consequences are always evil; when it serves a demented design, the passion of love is turned into the aggression of self-destruction.

The issue of sexual abuse and assault, especially the threat of rape, dominates the forsaken landscape of The Stand. On the novel's moral continuum, those individuals who choose to express themselves through a violent or dehumanized sexuality are Flagg's kindred. In contrast, the capacity to control sexual lust and violence—maintaining a responsibile attitude toward sexuality as a means for the expression of love—is related to the ability to resist evil and choose good.

At the opposite extreme of the self-control extolled by Glen Bateman and exemplified in Larry Underwood's final encounter with Nadine, King provides a group of immoral men who have used the collapse of civilization to indulge their hostility toward women. The four men who maintain "the zoo" have kidnapped eight women and hold them as sexual slaves. The sole purpose of this enterprise is the carnal gratification of the men involved; their captives are stripped of their humanity, reduced to orifices which are filled or tortured according to the daily whims of the men in charge: "'I'd get up in the morning, be raped two or three times, and then wait for Doc to hand out the pills,' said Susan matter-of-factly" (549). Using drugs to maintain female compliance, the "zoo keepers" resemble a retrogression toward primitive man that confirms Stu's worst fears about the dangers inherent in the abdication of civilized law. Ironically, the very nature of this travelling concubine—"the zoo"—suggests that the true beasts under discussion are not the unfortunates held in bondage, but rather their keepers.

In light of the close affiliation between sexuality and personality maintained throughout this novel, it is interesting that when the women in "the zoo" are liberated by Frannie, Harold, Glen, and Stu, their response toward the men who have mistreated them is to return violence for violence. Dayna Jurgens, Susan Stern, and Patty Kroger, in particular, behave in a manner that is decidedly "unfeminine," shattering one captor's head with the stock of a shotgun, violently squeezing another's crotch, and releasing "a long primeval scream of triumph that haunted Fran Goldsmith for the rest of her life" (544). Rape has forced "the zoo" women to break with traditional feminine behavior; to survive these vicious circumstances, they must act like men. Their experience in "the zoo" goes on to affect each of these women for the remainder of the novel. None of them ever fully recovers, as all are left incapable of divorcing sexuality from violence and deceit.

The men who operate "the zoo" are moving west when they encounter Frannie, Glen, Harold, and Stu. Their final destination is to join Flagg in Las Vegas, where no doubt they would be placed in charge of nightly entertainment at the MGM Grand. The same moral vacuum that inspired "the zoo" is likewise found in the municipal design already in place at Las Vegas. Each of these worlds features a realm of oppression—social and sexual—instigated by the strongest men and fortified by the power of technology. The denizens of Las Vegas are initially attracted to Flagg (for the same reason as they are also terrified of him) because he promises survival through technological domination; the men who operate "the zoo" similarly enforce their will over their captive women through administration of powerful pharmaceuticals.

In Flagg's city-state and in the parallel microcosm of "the zoo," women exist to satisfy the dark and salacious sexual urges of the men in control. Nadine Cross's artificially imposed virginity—insisted upon by Flagg and imposed at the expense of her natural and spontaneous emotions—is a condition analogous to the women who are held in bondage in "the zoo." The language used to describe Flagg's "seduction" of Cross is always suggestive of rape. Interestingly, he "enters" her for the first time in a kind of psychological rape—sustaining the novel's affiliation between rape and a conscious choice to perform evil—that occurs the moment after she elects to ignore the voice of her conscience in order to plant the bomb which will destroy the members of the Free Zone committee. Furthermore, the cold numbness and eventual catatonia Nadine experiences during and after Flagg's defilement is reminiscent of the chemically-induced impassivity and sexual stupefaction experienced by the women in "the zoo": "Nadine was blind, she was deaf, she was without a sense of touch. . . . And she felt him creep into her. A shriek built up within her, but she had no mouth with which to scream. *Penetration: entropy.* She didn't know what those words meant, put together like that; she only knew they were right" (860).

The Stand features some of the darkest aspects of King's critique of patriarchal domination. In It, the writer is critical of a male-oriented society that resorts to extreme levels of collective violence as its natural response to conflict or fear. In The Shining, the bloody history of the

116

Overlook Hotel, what Jack Torrance calls "an index of the whole post-World War II American character" (189), is cast in terms of patriarchal capitalism; the hotel's ghastly supernaturalism parallels and is modelled after the rise in influence of the American corporate state.[2] But in The Stand, we see King's perspective on the destructive nature of patriarchal domination expressed most explicitly through images of rape.

Most of the major events which occur in the novel—the choices which are made, the consequences which result from the actions initiated—are sexually motivated. Frannie and Stu begin to revivify their empty lives through the act of sexual intercourse: "Fran cried out her pleasure at the end of it, as her *good* orgasm burst through her" [italics mine] (559). In contrast, as Harold Lauder watches this healthy exchange from deep within the shadows, the seed of corruption is planted in him: "Neither of them saw Harold, as shadowy and as silent as the dark man himself, standing in the bushes and looking at them" (559). His next choice, to steal a look at her diary without permission, is another, metaphorical extension of the novel's rape imagery, as Harold violates both Frannie's trust and personal privacy. Lauder's spiral descent from a child-man with abundant potential to a decadent variation on the "zookeepers" and Flagg himself, emerges from the sexual jealousy he feels after uncovering Fran and Stu's union: "In the hour before dawn, he replaced the diary in Fran's pack and secured the buckles. He took no special precautions. If she woke, he thought coldly, he would kill her and then run. Run where? West. . . . He went back to his sleeping bag. He masturbated bitterly" (562).

If Lauder's moral poisoning begins with his reaction to Frannie's sexual involvement with Stu, his decadent interludes with Nadine solidify and refine his affiliation with evil. Not only does Nadine prey upon Harold's virginity, tempting him with promises of sensations never known, she likewise encourages his penchant for sexual perversion:

117

"'We can do things. Things you've never even
... no, I take that back. Maybe you *have* dreamed
of them, but you never dreamed you'd do them. We
can play. We can make ourselves drunk with it. We
can wallow in it. We can ...' She trailed off, and
then did look at him, a look so sly and sensual that
he felt himself stirring again. 'We can do anything—
everything—but that one little thing. And that one
little thing really isn't so important, is it?' Images
whirled giddily in his mind. Silk scarves ... boots.
.. leather ... rubber. Oh Jesus" (793).

It is important that Nadine's "one little thing" is forever denied to
Harold. The fact that Lauder technically dies a virgin, never having
actually participated in intercourse, serves to highlight his failure to
view sex as anything other than a self-enclosed act—its sole purpose,
his own physical release. As Nadine is willing to accommodate his
sexual fantasies primarily with her mouth, she becomes nothing more
than an extension of Harold's chronic urge to masturbate (as he does
even on the most inappropriate occasions, e.g. after reading Frannie's
journal). As such, their relationship serves Flagg's evil perfectly, as
the dark man thrives on human isolation and the pursuit of selfish
desires.

In a novel that fantasizes the abrupt dissolution of human civilization as we know it, and forces those who have survived into a
profoundly existential awareness of the human condition stripped
of social veneers, it is most appropriate that Stephen King should
distill his emphasis on the resulting cosmic struggle between good
and evil into the most personal and fundamental of human re-
sponses: sexuality. How a man or woman chooses to respond to
this issue is often the clearest indicator of his or her true nature.
People of good will gravitate toward sexual relationships that
mirror their personalities: nurturing, equal, responsive to others.
Correspondingly, the sexuality of evil is sterile and isolating.

When King's characters are seduced by the corruption of warped sexuality, it is symptomatic of moral vulnerability. Once they succumb, they eventually forfeit their identities and the ability to control their own destinies. After Flagg completes the violation he has ordained for Nadine by physically raping her in the desert, her soullessness is an extreme manifestation of what happens to every King character whose life is shaped by sexual perversion. As T.S. Eliot lamented the death of civilization through sexual encounters and inferences devoid of love in The Waste Land, King likewise suggests that humankind forsakes its connection to both God and man in the degradation of sexuality. In The Stand's fictional world, where characters must constantly adjust to circumstances which change as rapidly as the shifting strains of the superflu virus itself, King proposes counterpoints to such change in the existence of simple truths which endure and remain eternally operative in the realm of human affairs. As King reminds us in Danse Macabre, in words that are especially relevant to human interaction in The Stand, good will always be distinguishable from evil by virtue of its concern for the welfare of others: "Mortal man or woman [is] just another passenger in the boat, another pilgrim on the way to whatever there is. And if another pilgrim falls down [others must] help the fallen one off his or her feet, brush off his or her clothes, and see if he or she is all right, and able to go on. If such behavior is to be, it cannot be as a result of an intellectual moral stance; it is because there is such a thing as love, merely a practical fact, a practical force in human affairs. Morality is, after all, a codification of those things which the heart understands to be true and those things which the heart understands to be the demands of a life lived among others . . . civilization, in a word" (403).

Those characters in The Stand unable to resist sexual entrapment sever their connection to humanity and forge a link to evil. Flagg, Harold Lauder, The Kid, the "zookeepers," and others like them are modern versions of Adam after the Fall, who, instead of only losing the Garden of Eden, have also relinquished their self-respect, the love of Eve, and the hope of any reconciliation with God. Other characters—Stu Redman, Larry Underwood, Glen Bateman, and Frannie Goldsmith—who "understand the demands of life lived among others," demonstrate control over their sexual selves and behave in a manner that is both altruistic and moral. In this latter group, the truest model of human survival, we find the greatest hope for the future precisely because it has maintained contact with the greatest virtues from the past.

NOTES

1. As I have dealt with the subject of King's fictional women elsewhere, I will limit my discussion here. The interested reader should, however, examine chapters 3 and 7 in my book The Moral Voyages of Stephen King, Mercer Island, WA: Starmont House, 1989. Also insightful are Mary Pharr's essay "Partners in the Danse: Women in Stephen King's Fiction" in The Dark Descent: Essays Defining Stephen King's Horrorscape, ed. Tony Magistrale, Westport, CT: Greenwood Press, 1992; and Jackie Eller's essay "Wendy Torrance, One of King's Women: A Typology of King's Female Characters" in The Shining Reader, ed. Tony Magistrale, Mercer Island, WA: Starmont House, 1991.

2. For a more detailed explication of the nexus between the Overlook's powers and American patriarchy, the reader should consult the following sources: Patricia Ferreira, "Jack's Nightmare at the Overlook: The American Dream Inverted" and Alan Cohen, "The Collapse of Family and Language in Stephen King's The Shining." Both articles are found in The Shining Reader, ed. Tony Magistrale, Mercer Island, WA: Starmont House, 1991.

WORKS CITED

Cohen, Alan. "The Collapse of Language and Family in Stephen King's The Shining." The Shining Reader. Ed. Tony Magistrale. Mercer Island, WA: Starmont House, 1991.

Eller, Jackie. "Wendy Torrance, One of King's Women: A Typology of King's Female Characters." The Shining Reader. Ed. Tony Magistrale. Mercer Island, WA: Starmont House, 1991.

Ferreira, Patricia. "Jack's Nightmare at the Overlook: The American Dream Inverted." The Shining Reader. Ed. Tony Magistrale. Mercer Island, WA: Starmont House, 1991.

King, Stephen. Danse Macabre. New York: Everest House, 1981. The Shining. New York: Doubleday, 1977. The Stand. New York: NAL, 1991.

Magistrale, Anthony. The Moral Voyages of Stephen King. Mercer Island, WA: Starmont House, 1989.

Pharr, Mary. "Partners in the Danse: Women in Stephen King's Fiction." The Dark Descent: Essays Defining Stephen King's Horrorscape. Ed. Tony Magistrale. Westport, CT: Greenwood Press, 1992.

Terrell, Carroll F.. Stephen King: Man and Artist. Orono, Maine: Northern Lights Publishing Company, 1990.

Underwood, Tim and Chuck Miller, eds.. Bare Bones: Conversations on Terror with Stephen King. New York: McGraw-Hill, 1988.

CHAPTER SEVEN

Choice, Sacrifice, Destiny, and Nature in The Stand

Bernadette Lynn Bosky

Numerous critics have remarked that The Stand is Stephen King's most popular novel, especially—but not exclusively—among teenagers (see Reino, 65; Herron, 131). In his book on the first decade of King's career, Joseph Reino expresses surprise, and more than a little disapproval, that "the more brilliantly crafted "Night Surf" (based on precisely the same theme) does not seem to attract similar youthful enthusiasm." King's earlier short story, Reino concludes, "perhaps moves . . . too quickly and too close to the uncomfortable truth of universal selfishness and indifference to the sufferings of others" (65). Reino's statements can be argued in many ways: it is debatable, for instance, whether "Night Surf" really is "more brilliantly crafted" than The Stand; or whether, apart from the shared plot-device of the superflu, the two works are thematically the same, or even similar. Most of all, the "uncomfortable truth of universal selfishness and indifference to the sufferings of others" may be more obvious to some than to others.

If that principle is so taken for granted that no other view can produce good art, then The Stand is bad art. In this way, The Stand is thematically the opposite of "Night Surf," which does show the prevalence of cruelty and indifference in a world without hope. On the other hand, The Stand is, in King's own words, "inherently optimistic . . . a testament to the enduring values of courage, kindness, friendship, and love" as well as a novel rife with horror (Playboy interview, 24-25). While "Night Surf" is about the inevitability of endings, The Stand constantly reinforces the necessity of making new beginnings. "Night Surf" takes place in an amoral universe in which one might as well be cruel, while the events of The Stand consistently show the rewards of kindness (including the ultimate kindness, deliberate sacrifice for communal good) and inevitable defeat of selfishness.

Which position will seem more "true" is, of course, up to the reader. What is undeniable is that many readers find The Stand to be both credible and reassuring in its worldview, a combination they cherish. Elsewhere, I have discussed this characteristic of King's work in general: "his fiction shows us an image of ourselves and our world that we want to believe, and find we can believe—at least for as long as we join him in his books" (237). Nowhere is this more true than in The Stand. Don Herron reports one teenager's explanation of why The Stand is her favorite book by King: "it presented a positive picture of humanity—there may be hate, fear, and the threat of nuclear war, but there are a lot of okay people . . . trying to do the best they know how" (152). Moreover, the optimism of The Stand goes beyond the personalities of the characters, to implicit rules that govern the events of the novel. The deaths of good people still occur, and are still tragic, but the sorrow is reduced or justified, usually by positive consequences that would not otherwise have come about. Those who have chosen the "dark" side, on the other hand, pay for that choice in credible and proportionate ways, punished not so much for their sins as by them. Part of King's accomplishment in The Stand is to present the reassurance of traditional values in new ways, capable of convincing a new, largely secular popular audience.

One of the paradoxes of The Stand is that so many readers can find so much hope in a book so dominated by death. In a sense, the death of 99.4% of the human race, from the government-engineered "superflu," is only the beginning. Of the survivors whom we get to know and care about in The Stand, many—probably a majority—are dead before the novel ends. Among major characters, the percentage is even higher: Stu Redman, Fran Goldsmith, Tom Cullen, Lucy Swann, and Leo Rockway are left to mourn Larry Underwood, Glen Bateman, Ralph Brentner, Dayna Jurgens, Judge Farris, Sue Stern, Nick Andros, Mother Abagail—and, of course, Nadine Cross, Harold Lauder, and everyone else on the Dark Man's side, many of whom are depicted very sympathetically despite their wrong choices. What matters most, however, is not the number of deaths in The Stand but how they are handled and what novel-specific worldview the reader can infer. By how the deaths happen and what happens as a result, King creates a sense of optimism. In The Stand, he makes the fates of his characters credible and satisfying expressions of an inherently moral universe, in which—despite the deaths of people we can like, understand, and even identify with—the good still outweighs the bad.

In his introduction to the new, enlarged edition, Stephen King calls The Stand "this long tale of dark Christianity" (xii). The issue of Christianity in The Stand presents interesting problems, especially considering the generally negative depiction of organized religion in King's work. (See Reino, 51; Larson, 106-108; Magistrale, 36-38; and Grant, 146-147.) The Stand lacks the negative depiction of organized Christianity found in King's works from Carrie forward; on the other hand, it does so by having little to say about organized religion at all. In The Stand, King seems to draw a distinction between institutional religion and personal spiritual experience, and to concentrate entirely on the latter. For instance, among the many survivors of the superflu, any kind of religious leaders at all—priest, minister, or rabbi—are conspicuous by their absence. (Thanks to Robert Shea for this insight.) One conclusion we can certainly draw, however, is that The Stand presents a worldview which, like Christianity, includes the virtue and efficacy of voluntary individual sacrifice.

First of all, self-sacrifice is primarily the personal choice, freely made, only of those who are already on the side of benevolent community, represented by Mother Abagail and the Denver Free Zone. In no case is a fatal outcome absolutely certain, and in most cases the characters still express hopes for survival. However, all choices do clearly involve risk, sometimes including the near-certainty of death. This combination, for example, is conveyed in Glen Bateman's accepting but darkly ironic statement:

"After fifty years of confirmed agnosticism, it
seems to be my fate to follow an old black woman's
God into the jaws of death. If that's my fate, then
that's my fate. End of story. But I'd rather walk than
ride, when you get right down to it. Walking takes
longer, consequently I live longer for a few days,
anyway." (1037-1038)

This risk is chosen because with it comes the hope of helping others. Sometimes the possible benefits are obvious, while other times
they are less clear, a matter of intuition and faith. Most importantly,
in the universe of The Stand, such expectations are always fulfilled,
although often not in the way that the person making the sacrifice had
expected.

Perhaps the most obvious example of this process is the death and
helpful afterlife of Nick Andros, the deaf-mute who—along with Stu
Redman and Larry Underwood—serves King as an Everyman hero,
until his death from the bomb planted by Nadine Cross and Harold
Lauder. Like Fran Goldsmith, Nick experiences a sharp intuition of
the bomb's presence, just before it goes off; he pushes Fran away but
dives after the bomb instead of following her, presumably hoping to
reach the explosives in time to prevent detonation and save lives (890).
Thus, though the situation was not of Nick's construction, his sacrifice is intentional—a common pattern in The Stand. Since he does not
reach the bomb in time, it may at first seem that his death has accomplished nothing. However, King challenges this view, soon enough,
by Mother Abagail's mysterious statement, "although not all of Nick
is gone yet, it seems to me. No, not all" (917). By this time, the readers—like the characters—have learned the reliability of her pro-
nouncements, so the effect is one of further hope.

Indeed, in a way that the agnostic Nick would not have anticipated,
his death eventually saves two lives, as it frees Nick's spirit to guide
Tom Cullen, his mentally retarded friend, through dreams. First, when
Julie Lawry recognizes Tom as a potential spy from the Free Zone,

Nick warns Tom to avoid search-parties, both telling Tom to leave the main road and providing him with alternate landmarks to follow home (1011-1013). Thus, Tom survives to discover and help Stu Redman, prevented by a broken leg from completing his own expedition to Las Vegas (1093). The second consequences of Nick's sacrifice are revealed in one of the most touching scenes in The Stand, as the ghost-Nick guides Tom to a pharmacy and instructs him in what he must do to save Stu's life, endangered by pneumonia (1106-1107). Nick's guidance in this case depends not only on his death, which allows him to appear to Tom in dreams and to speak to him (as he could not in life), but also on his earlier suffering and near-death from a leg infection (368-375, 1106-1107).

Tom's dreams could be due to some other mechanism, so that he would have been able to save his own life and Stu's even if Nick had not died. In fact, Stu does not at first believe that Nick helped Tom in the pharmacy (1107), and his final verdict is, "I don't know how you picked the right pills . . . if it was Nick or God or just plain old luck, but you did it" (1122). However, while King leaves other possibilities open, they never seem fully explanatory. When Tom hears of Nick's death, he replies, "I'm going to see him in heaven . . . And he'll be able to talk and I'll be able to think" (1095). The overwhelming likelihood is that this meeting has happened before Tom's death, partly because of the selfless nature of Nick's.

In fact, King may also hint of a final consequence of Nick's death, if some suggestions are construed in certain ways. Tom seems both brighter and more adult when the novel concludes than he did before his ordeal: this is remarked upon by Stu (1093-1094) and by Tom himself, who feel it may be time for him to put away childish things (1017). It is also demonstrated in Tom's switch from spelling everything M-O-O-N to spelling "OK" out as "O-and-K" (1099) and the even more sophisticated, "C-I-T-Y-L-I-M-I-T-S, that spells Boulder, laws, yes" (1129). This development may be due to Tom's various experiences, including his own higher self—"God's Tom"—being awakened by hypnosis (817-822). If that is the case, Tom's increased ability and maturity may result from his own adventures—and suffering—in the cause of the Free Zone. However, Tom's development may also come from his communion with Nick's spirit; certainly, it begins at the same time. Moreover, in the pharmacy-vision Nick tells Tom, "For God's sake, be a man!" and Tom vows to try (1106-1107). In either case, virtuous sacrifice has been rewarded.

Nick's death and return are sometimes (among other resonances) suggestive of the Biblical Jesus, such as when he shows his scar to Tom (1106), like Christ demonstrating his wounds to the disciple Thomas. Another Biblical echo occurs when Mother Abagail, spiritual leader of the Free Zone, withdraws into the wilderness without sustenance. Seeking atonement for her own sin and clear guidance for her community, Abagail accomplishes that and more, at the cost of her life.

To most readers, Abagail's sacrifice and triumph works less well than Nick's, for any of a number of reasons. King admits that he had trouble with her character (Playboy interview, 38). Although he tries to render her credible through doubts and weakness, these are usually overcome by acceptance too easily and quickly (503, 513, 521-523), especially when compared to the more familiar struggles and doubts of Nick, Fran Goldsmith, Larry Underwood, and others. Moreover, Abagail's major battle is with pride, which distracts her as she greets Nadine Cross (657-662) and forces her to leave Boulder in order to pray and fast (717-720). King does try to demonstrate a difference between this false pride and the honest satisfaction that Abagail takes in her abilities and accomplishments, such as when she sung in the Grange Hall as a child (486-487); still, pride is no longer a fashionable enemy, and Abagail's reparations for it can seem excessive, even superfluous and self-destructive. Events of The Stand make clear, however, that her fatal sacrifice is ultimately worthwhile.

Most obviously, Mother Abagail's return from the wilderness—led by a little child, the sometimes-psychic Leo Rockway (898)—

happens exactly in time to attract attention during the fatal committee-meeting: most people, going outside to investigate the commotion, are saved from the bomb that Nadine Cross and Harold Lauder had planted inside (898). "It's like a miracle," King does not resist pointing out through Stu Redman (897), who perhaps speaks more truly than he then knows. More subtly, her ordeal is necessary for Abagail to complete her role as spiritual leader of the Free Zone. After her return, Abagail is physically depleted but spiritually charged, completely a vehicle for divine guidance. She demonstrates knowledge she could not have gained naturally, such as the deaths of Nick Andros and Susan Stern (913), Fran's pregnancy (916), and Glen Bateman's earlier words about the dark man (919); she also heals Frannie's whiplash as a "sign" (918). On her deathbed, Abagail conveys all that she knows about the necessary trip west, presenting what she feels are God's plans for Stu Redman, Larry Underwood, Ralph Brentner and Glen Bateman (917-920).

Her condition—as a near-dead instrument of higher forces—is essential in two ways. First, the four pilgrims were more likely to agree to journey west because of the clearly unusual nature of Abagail's ordeal, and because of both the supernatural abilities and natural arguments with which she returns. This is less true of Ralph, who almost certainly would have gone anyway; but even he receives reassurance (920), and Glen (919) and Stu (921) are clearly convinced and changed by the final interview. (Larry's agreement is much more clear than his reasons (920).) Second, the reader finds out later that Randall Flagg, the dark man, was inexplicably unable to see Abagail's final moments, including any possible plans against him—a fact which disturbs him deeply (980-981). One is reminded of the inability of Flagg's traveling third eye to "see" Tom Cullen, because of Tom's mental retardation (1009). The similarity between Tom and Abagail on her deathbed, King hints, is that both have lost self in a way that leaves them fully open to the numinous (821, 1044, 1046-1047). Given this, Abagail's final period of fasting and prayer is necessary, so that the journey west can be completed without Flagg's knowledgeable intervention. As Lloyd Henreid says, speaking of his bossman Flagg, "Everything was going so good, right up to the night he came in and said the old lady was dead over there in the Free Zone. He said the last obstacle was out of our way. But that's when things started to get funny" (1028).

Of course, the characters who most clearly choose to sacrifice themselves for the good of others are those members of the Free Zone who voluntarily travel west, to suffer and survive—as Stu Redman and Tom Cullen do—or, more often, to die. Dayna Jurgens and Judge Farris go to Las Vegas as spies; Ralph, Glen, and Larry follow, on a journey in which the specific goal is as unclear as its importance seems clear. In each case, the character's death is still tragic, but associated with optimistic implications that the death serves a purpose. The effects of the deaths, whether as final as the nuclear holocaust or as seemingly minor as a blow against Flagg's confidence, all lead inevitably to the fall of the dark man and safety for the Free Zone—if only, as Stu Redman says, "For a little while" (1137).

While the deaths of the Judge and Dayna accomplish the least, they are still important, especially in the latter case. Judge Farris's fate is literally the beginning of the end for Flagg. The first event in The Stand in which Flagg's will is thwarted, and the first sign of his inevitable decline, comes when Farris's head, which Flagg had wanted to send to the Free Zone as a warning, is damaged beyond recognition. Flagg punishes Bobby Terry, the agent responsible, but the act is irreversible (942-943). Dayna, identified as a spy and interrogated by the dark man himself, kills herself rather than reveal the identity of the other spy in Las Vegas, which Flagg intuits she does know (964-965). Obviously, her death has the literally vital result of concealing Tom Cullen's identity until he is out of the city—thus perpetuating a chain of mutual aid that saves not only Tom, but also Stu Redman. Moreover, Dayna's death, like that of the Judge, undermines Flagg's confidence and control. His initial rage at being cheated by Dayna is infantile, violent, and petty, betraying an inherent weakness in Flagg (965). When Flagg begins to doubt himself and the certainty of his victory over the Free Zone, he thinks about "the troubling matter of the spies. The

Judge, with his head blown off. The girl, who had eluded him at the last second" (981).

King further softens the effect of their deaths on the reader by making clear that both the Judge and Dayna are living on borrowed time and know it, even apart from their lives being spared by superflu immunity. The Judge is almost not sent west because he is too old (709, 810), and he is kept off of the slate for the "temporary" central committee for that reason (701); his death is also a release from arthritis and other suffering (941). Even more strikingly, both Dayna Jurgens and Sue Stern (who dies in the explosion of Harold and Nadine's bomb) are alive only because of the actions of Stu Redman and other Free Zone members, a debt which they acknowledge. In a sub-plot largely cut from the earlier edition of The Stand, Stu and his party rescue Dayna, Sue, and other women from a pack of murderous rapists (551-561). Explaining Dayna's willingness to go to Las Vegas as a spy, Sue tells Stu, "For one thing, she reminded me that if we'd stayed with those men . . . we would have wound up dead or in the West anyway, because that's the direction they were going in" (842). By emphasizing the conditional nature of the Judge's and Dayna's lives, King can have all the tragic emotional impact from their deaths, without the pessimistic flavor carried, for instance, by Tad Trenton's death in Cujo or the ever-mounting human deaths in Pet Sematary.

In a climax that some readers find emotionally satisfying and some call an implausible *deus ex machina*—and, no doubt, some react to in both ways—the deaths of Larry Underwood and Ralph Brentner literally set the stage for the atomic holocaust that ends Flagg's immediate threat to the Free Zone. Most obviously, the place of their intended execution draws together the Trashcan Man's atomic offering and the spark, generated by Flagg, that sets it off (1082-1085). Ralph and Larry are, however, more important than that, affecting the action directly as well as providing the occasion. The fact that viewing of the execution is mandatory for all Las Vegas residents (1074, 1076, 1080)—like the crucifixion of Hector Drogan earlier in The Stand (623-625)—causes the presence of Whitney Horgan, already disaffected with Flagg and planning to escape (1028-1030, 1072-1073). To this extent, as in other ways, Flagg advances his own downfall. However, it is also possible, and even likely, that Whitney speaks out due to the example and rhetoric of Larry and Ralph.

King repeatedly implies that Larry's "stand" on the Las Vegas stage is his final performance, the fulfillment—and joining—of his new life and the old life he had erroneously sought to disavow. This is shown by Larry's dreams, in which confrontation with Flagg takes the form of a rock show (1060-1061, 1062); and by his "queer feeling that it was a performance, a show to be played" (1063)—which indeed it is, literally (1077). When Larry addresses the crowds, "his voice, trained by years of singing, rolled out of his chest with surprising strength." Ralph, without Larry's professional force but with even more spiritual insight, hints at Flagg's non-human, eternal nature: "Flagg's not your name! . . . Why don't you tell em your real name?" Both utterances are literally prophetic, spoken with accuracy and spiritual force, and the crowd is audibly affected (1079). When Whitney speaks, attempting to likewise move the crowd's conscience, his words even resemble Larry's: "This ain't right! . . . You know it ain't!" (1080), a less eloquent echo of Larry Underwood's "You people know this is wrong! . . . I don't expect you to stop it, but I do expect you to remember it!" (1079). When Whitney speaks, Flagg gruesomely kills him with "a blue ball of fire" (1082), which then ignites the Trashcan Man's atomic bomb (1084-1085).

Thus, as Michael Collings states, "The Walkin Dude is not defeated in a single moment, with the single flash of a nuclear device," but "is instead defeated . . . by the small actions of individuals choosing properly" (88). The events come about, one after the other, like a line of falling dominoes. Without Whitney's moment of choice and conscience, Flagg would not have provided the supernatural spark that detonated the bomb; without the sacrifice of Larry and Ralph, Whitney might not have spoken up, and probably would not have been anywhere near the atomic bomb; and without Mother Abagail's voluntary ordeal and death, Larry and Ralph would not have journeyed to Las Vegas at all.

Glen Bateman may seem, in some sense, wasted. Since his death occurs the night before the scheduled public execution, Bateman—despite his journey—is not even present on the apocalyptic stage. However, his fate is more comparable to the deaths of Dayna Jurgens and Judge Farris than to those of Larry and Ralph. First, like them, he delivers a serious blow to the dark man's sense of confidence and purpose: he laughs at Flagg, an intolerable reaction which is avenged but not forgotten when Glen is shot. Lloyd Henreid, Flagg's assistant, also reacts to the shooting—and Glen Bateman's calm dignity—in a way that suggests a serious challenge to the Las Vegas government in the future, had the Las Vegas settlement had a future (1071-1072). Beyond that, King softens the impact of Glen Bateman's death, as he does with those of Dayna and the Judge. In prison, Larry suspects that Glen is already dead and thinks, "Well, he had been old, his arthritis had been paining him, and whatever Flagg had planned for them this morning was apt to be very unpleasant" (1074-1075).

Often in The Stand, the efficacious self-sacrifice for others is also a personal triumph; when the character has time for final thoughts before the end, they show calm acceptance and a deep peace concerning both what has happened and what is yet to come. This is probably true of Dayna (965) and possibly true of the Judge (941). Abagail dies at peace with herself, assured and assuring the four pilgrims she sends out, "With God's help you will stand" (919). Glen's final writing is not a sociological treatise, but a "proverb—or was it an aphorism?" on the prison wall, affirming both his own "intrinsic worth" and his acceptance of himself as the tool of a higher purpose (1069). The most obvious moment of resolution and healing, however, belongs to Larry Underwood, who has the most need of it—at least among Abagail's followers:

> . . . He had been
> (thinking? praying?)

It was all the same thing. Whichever it had been,
the old wound in himself had finally closed, leaving
him at peace. He had felt the two people that he had
been all his life—the real one and the ideal one—
merge into one living being . . . I'm going to die. If
there's a God—and now I believe there must be—
that's His will. We're going die and somehow all of
this will end as a result of our dying. (1074)

Like Ralph Brentner, who feels fear but never loses faith, Larry
prepares himself for death with the litany, "I will fear no evil" (1076,
1082, 1085). (This line from the 23rd Psalm forms a refrain in The
Stand. It is also spoken—in "a peculiar" reply to a question from Stu
Redman—by Glen Bateman (1038); and Tom Cullen offers a frac-
tured version of the same Psalm (1017).) When Ralph realizes their
approaching fate, his "face was transported in a terrible joy. His eyes
shone" (1084).

While the self-sacrifice of Mother Abagail and her followers
paradoxically leads to fulfillment, Flagg and his followers seek to
assert themselves above any other value—love, community, destiny—
but end up empty, often deprived of even their humanity. This is especially true of Flagg. As Douglas E. Winter observes, "He is a rheto-
rician of self, seemingly obsessed with convincing himself and others of his importance and destiny" (61) despite—or perhaps because
of—his suppressed awareness that his true nature is a self-defeating
negation. As Tony Magistrale writes, evil in King's fiction "tends to
annihilate not only its opposite but itself" (65). Certainly, Flagg's very
being is so destructive that it can best be defined by negatives.
Throughout The Stand, Mother Abagail and her followers show they
understand this. Dayna, thinking of the way in which Flagg's followers are too afraid to even mention his name, refers to Flagg as "the great
There/Not There" (945); Abagail realizes "that behind the conscious
evil there was an unconscious blackness," a void which could not create but only uncreate (653). Under hypnosis, Tom Cullen describes the

dark man, again primarily by negatives, "He's always outside. He came out of time. He doesn't know himself. He's afraid of us. We're inside. He knows magic. He can call wolves and live in the crows. He's the king of nowhere. But he's afraid of us. He's afraid of inside," (818). Finally, even Flagg realizes that in order to reach his goals as the Walkin Dude, "He was losing himself"—losing his memories, his powers of thought, his choices, and his humanity, "like an onion, slowly peeling away one layer at a time" (982).

Critics have noticed that in The Stand, the forces of good are more closely tied to humanity than are those of evil, as is especially clear in the contrast between Mother Abagail and the dark man, Randall Flagg (Notkin 136, Collings 86). This may, as Notkin suggests, be a flaw in the development of The Stand (137); however, it can also be seen as an inevitable outgrowth of the novel's philosophy. First, this approach to good and evil locates King in the mainstream of Christian thought, both in the paradox that we only keep what we let go, and also—as James L. Hicks notes of the "vacant but seductive Marsten House" in 'Salem's Lot—in the idea that "evil is a hollow emptiness, as St. Augustine repeatedly explains" (80). Second, King seems to imply a specific spiritual and psychological mechanism by which certain choices inevitably erode a character's humanity. As Magistrale has noted, evil in the fiction of Stephen King "can establish dominion only at the expense of the individual's moral conscience" (65). Yet this conscience is a deep part of the soul; to silence it, characters must perform a kind of moral lobotomy, excising the best parts of themselves, until what is left becomes less than human. During the final confrontation in Las Vegas, the voices of conscience reiterate that what they're saying is already known to the audience (1080, 1075-1076, 1079). In the world of The Stand, moral insight is natural, and its denial takes a self-abnegating act of will.

The Stand depicts moral decay as a series of small decisions; although each bad choice makes the next more likely, a different direction could be taken at any time—a fact which Flagg's followers try to deny, although they know it to be true. I have elsewhere examined the clearest example of this process, in the character of Harold Lauder. The same degeneration, freely chosen at every major cusp, is enacted by Flagg's "wife," Nadine Cross, and by his associates Lloyd Henreid and (especially in the new, longer version of The Stand) Donald Mervin Elbert.

Just as Randall Flagg becomes nothing but the dark man, then darkness, and then not even that, Elbert feels himself voluntarily eroding until only the Trashcan Man remains (577, 622-623, 626); even then, Trashcan Man experiences one final "moment of choice," but his devotion to the dark man and his own desire for "the lovely explosions . . . the lovely fires" lead him to choose wrongly (1021). He literally embraces his destruction, struggling to bring the atomic warhead back to Las Vegas (1032-1033); it is important to note that his personal death from radiation sickness would have been assured, even if "the hand of God" had not intervened (1083-1085). The Trashcan Man shows intense—literally religious—dedication to Flagg, a good character trait in the service of a bad cause. Thus, he wins the readers' sympathy, but not our approval, and his death is sad and horrifying but just. Similarly, the tenacious loyalty of Project Blue's officer William Starkey, who almost certainly would have joined Flagg's side if he had survived his own project's superflu, causes untold added deaths before he himself commits suicide (130-134, 175-179). The material in the longer edition of The Stand, describing Starkey's motives and fate, render him more human and compelling, but no more correct or admirable.

Flagg's other main assistant, Lloyd Henreid, presents an interesting combination of virtues and vices, reasons and rationalizations. Like the Trashcan Man, Lloyd shows an honest dedication to Flagg, including deserved gratitude for rescuing him from starvation and worse. However, burdened by sanity as the Trashcan Man is not, Lloyd has doubts about his allegiance (362-363, 1005, 1010, 1028-1029); and whenever possible, Lloyd silences these doubts with reminders of how much he owes Flagg (367-368, 1005, 1029- 1030). Thus, Lloyd's expressions of gratitude, while genuine, clearly are also ways for him to manage his doubts without having to act on them by making a new choice. (This is also true of Harold Lauder's belief that it is "already too late" for him to change direction—see Bosky, 228.) Henreid also has other motives for following Flagg, which show him in a less sympathetic light: hatred and a desire for revenge on those who have wronged him (360-361, 366-367); the "pleasure of being *chosen*" (366); and the increased intelligence and authority which Flagg has lent him (1029-1030). Ultimately, Lloyd's dedication and gratitude are partly ways to disavow responsibility for his own actions, first blaming his partner-in-crime Poke (277, 364) and then finding an even more murderous direction in affiliation with Flagg. Lloyd may occasionally fool himself, but he does not fool the reader: Lloyd's doom was as freely chosen as were those of Starkey, the Trashcan Man, Harold Lauder, and Nadine Cross.

Harold and Nadine both betray the Boulder Free Zone and cross over—as Nadine's last name suggests (Collings, 87)—to the dark man's side. This presents King with a special challenge: creating characters of sufficient ambiguity to lend credibility to both allegiances. The reader must always believe that the characters have enough good in them to make redemption constantly possible, yet also must believe Harold and Nadine's continued downward choices in the face of mounting awareness of the horrors that await them. King depicts an all-too-credible process of self-chosen damnation in Harold's case, fueled by pride and anger and perpetuated by deliberate isolation from the Boulder community (Bosky, 227-230; Magistrale, 63-64). In the case of Nadine Cross, the artistic problem is more demanding and the results are more contradictory.

Nadine chooses to be Flagg's bride, but she also is chosen by him while she is still innocent, in a way that is not true of any other character in The Stand (637, 777-782). Flagg also robs her of her final chance for remorse. Stricken with guilt over the bomb she and Harold have planted, Nadine actually "stopped thinking she would turn around and go back"; but before she can do that (or, like Harold or the Trashcan Man, deliberately pass up this final opportunity) she is lit-

137

erally possessed by the dark man, rendering moot any moral decision on her part (873-874). On the other hand, sometimes Nadine is shown making moral choices, and they are always the wrong ones. Like Lloyd, Nadine tries to blame others for her choices: "So you see, none of this is my fault. *None* of it!" she says to the boy, Leo (836). However, Leo—and the reader—knows that Nadine doth protest too much, and that she deliberately waited to ask Larry Underwood for help, until she knew it was too late (858). When Leo says, "It's like *he's* rubbing away the part of her brain that knows right from wrong" (858), does he describe a deliberate choice, a process which Nadine could not avoid, or both? When Flagg tells Nadine, "It's much too late to say no, dear," is that more rationalization (and, in this case, intimidation) or a factual statement? Even King may not be certain.

In keeping with this ambiguity in Nadine's character, King essentially provides her with two fates. The first, commensurate with the villainy of her acts if they are freely chosen, may be the most gruesome end of any character in The Stand. Driven mad by intercourse with Flagg (in which she sees his true self), Nadine's shell is left: a drooling incubator for Flagg's child, comatose except for compulsive masturbation and enough awareness to shudder at Flagg's touch (988, 1005-1006, 1010). Yet something remains, and later revives; Nadine appears, looking "like some pallid deranged Sybil" and declaring Flagg's approaching doom (1015). Flagg throws Nadine to her death, realizing too late that her end—very much like Dayna's—was a deliberate attempt to thwart the dark man's plans. This time the damage is even greater, and so are Flagg's fury and feelings of impending doom (1016-1017).

Harold Lauder's death also carries dual implications, but in a more coherent and artistically satisfying way. He pays for his crimes physically, when an accident caused by Flagg deposits him in a gorge, injured and alone, without food or water (973-974). The traitor to the Free Zone has been betrayed by Flagg, a connection that Nadine makes explicit (975); rejecting society when it welcomed him, Harold faces death afraid and alone. (Similarly, Flagg ensures a grisly fate for the

Kid (587-615), who abuses the most selfless of the dark man's servants (598- 600, 611-612) and plans to depose Flagg himself (591-592).) However, the lengthy ordeal provides Harold Lauder with time to reach personal insight and a kind of emotional triumph, achieved through writing. At first, Harold attempts to justify himself as he has throughout his journal, writing, "I was misled" (977). This is the same abdication of responsibility that characterizes Lloyd, Nadine (some of the time), and Harold's own past. Immediately, however, Harold admits the threadbare nature of his excuse and his own evident hypocrisy; he signs his journal "Hawk," the name that he "could not accept" when it was given to him in Boulder but which he finally "take[s] freely." Although he shoots himself, Harold does, as he realizes, achieve "a little sanity and maybe even a little dignity" at the end (977-979).

Finally, the destinies of Flagg and his followers are portrayed by King as morally and artistically justified, the inevitable results of choices that were made freely and with at least some intuition of the consequences. If the voluntary sacrifices by Abagail and her group can be viewed as prepayment for future grace, the fates of Flagg's followers generally involve the unwilling but necessary payment of past-due bills, knowingly incurred. Moreover, in the worldview of The Stand, acceptance of one's nature and destiny lead, if not to survival, at least to final peace of mind. This is seen consistently among Mother Abagail and her followers, in the final assertion of Nadine's and Harold's best selves, and—a stunning exception that still, somehow, seems right— in the death of Flagg's utterly insane and utterly selfless follower, the Trashcan Man.

Innocent characters in The Stand do die by blind chance, certainly including most of those who die from the superflu, which "mostly was just a thing that happened" (31-32). Perhaps the best post-flu example is the death of a minor character named Mark, who dies of a burst appendix not long before he would have reached Mother Abagail (526-531, 538-544). However, this episode primarily provides verisimilitude, without seriously challenging the pattern of the novel. Furthermore, immediately following Mark's death, his lover, Perion, kills herself. With Peri's suicide, the tragedy of the event is reinforced, but so is the implied worldview of The Stand: like Rita Blakemoor (237-241, 299-313, 319-322, and especially 376- 380), Peri finds that the new world is not kind to those who cannot take their stand in it—a stand that must be taken independently, if not absolutely alone. Even the chapter concerning the second wave of deaths after the superflu ("the unkindest cut of all, some might have said" (350)) alternates the accidental deaths of innocents (350-351, 355, 357) with accounts of intentional or semi-intentional suicide (353-355), a heroin addict's fatal overdose (357-358), and the ironically appropriate deaths of two women whom King clearly presents as repugnant by any humane standards (351-353, 356-367). As the refrain of that chapter puts it, "No great loss" (352, 355, 358).

Stephen King clearly can be, as Samuel Schuman puts it, "a rather stern moralist" who presents "voyeuristic thrills at some fairly gruesome incidents" which are "packaged within a thematic structure which reinforces main-line Western moral traditions" (108, 113). In The Stand, perhaps more than any other of his novels, King combines the appeal of fictional thrills with both the demands and the reassurance of a consistent worldview. It is one thing for an author to assert that appropriate sacrifice is rewarded and immoral choices are inherently self-defeating; it is quite another thing—and a far more difficult one—for an author to present a work in which those tenets consistently and credibly manifest themselves in the nature and destinies of all of the major characters. As we have seen, that is precisely what King sets out to do, and largely accomplishes, in that "long tale of dark Christianity," The Stand.

WORKS CITED

Bosky, Bernadette Lynn. "The Mind's a Monkey: Character and Psychology In Stephen King's Recent Fiction." Kingdom of Fear: The World of Stephen King. Eds. Tim Underwood and Chuck Miller. New York: New American Library, 1986: 209-238.

Collings, Michael R. "The Stand: Science Fiction Into Fantasy." Discovering Stephen King. Ed. Darrell Schweitzer. Mercer Island, Washington: Starmont House, Inc., 1985: 83-90.

Grant, Charles L. "The Grey Arena." Fear Itself: The Horror Fiction of Stephen King. Eds. Tim Underwood and Chuck Miller. San Francisco: Underwood-Miller, 1982: 145-151.

Herron, Don. "King: The Good, the Bad, and the Academic." Kingdom of Fear: The World of Stephen King. Eds. Tim Underwood and Chuck Miller. New York: New American Library, 1986: 129-157.

Hicks, James L. "Stephen King's Creation of Horror in 'Salem's Lot: A Prolegomenom Towards a New Hermeneutic of the Gothic Novel." The Gothic World of Stephen King: Landscape of Nightmares. Eds. Gary Hoppenstand and Ray B. Browne. Bowling Green, Ohio: Bowling Green State University Popular Press, 1987: 75-83.

King, Stephen. "The Playboy Interview, Conducted by Eric Norden." The Stephen King Companion. Ed. George Beahm. Kansas City and New York: Andrews and McMeel, 1989: 19-45. The Stand. Revised Edition. New York: Doubleday, 1990.

Larson, Randall D. "Cycle of the Werewolf and the Moral Tradition of Horror." Discovering Stephen King. Ed. Darrell Schweitzer. Mercer Island, Washington: Starmont House, Inc., 1985: 102-108.

Magistrale, Tony. Landscape of Fear: Stephen King's American Gothic. Bowling Green, Ohio: Bowling Green State University Popular Press, 1988.

Notkin, Deborah L. "Stephen King: Horror and Humanity for Our Time." Fear Itself: The Horror Fiction of Stephen King. Ed. Tim Underwood and Chuck Miller. San Francisco: Underwood-Miller, 1982: 131-142.

Reino, Joseph. Stephen King: The First Decade, Carrie to Pet Sematary. Boston: Twayne Publishers/G.K. Hall & Co., 1988.

Schuman, Samual. "Taking Stephen King Seriously: Reflections on a Decade of Best-Sellers." The Gothic World of Stephen King: Landscape of Nightmares. Ed. Gary Hoppenstand and Ray B. Browne. Bowling Green, Ohio: Bowling Green State University Popular Press, 1987: 107-114.

Winter, Douglas E. Stephen King: The Art of Darkness. Revised and Expanded. New York and Scarborough, Ontario: New American Library/A Plume Book, 1986.

CHAPTER EIGHT

Dark Streets and Bright Dreams
Rationalism, Technology, and "Impossible Knowledge"
Stephen King's The Stand

Michael A. Morrison

There's so much we'll never know. But then, why
would we want to?
—Fran Goldsmith in The Stand by Stephen King

Ruled by rationalism and awash in gadgets, our society tends to
neglect the moral questions that attend the inexorable march of technology. Confident that we can control whatever we create, we blithely
drive forward the engine of technology, as vulnerable now as Victor
Frankenstein was in Mary Shelley's early 19th century admonitory
Gothic. Such, at any rate, is the argument of The Stand, Stephen King's
vast novel of cataclysm, confrontation, and rebirth in which technological hubris catalyzes an apocalypse of Biblical proportion, clearing
the slate for the return of the irrational.

As a philosophical stance, irrationalism has taken quite a beating
in the technoculture. Most influential pundits and many of us mere
citizens value rationalism and reason, logic and the scientific method,
gadgets and technology, over dreams and hunches. To a scientist, a
technocrat, or most other late 20th-century rationalists, knowledge
obtained through such irrational means as telepathy, precognition,
clairvoyance, contact with the spirit world, or dreams is suspect, spe-
cious, "impossible." The behavioral norms of some sub-cultures dero-
gate even so innocuous an irrational mode as intuition. Perhaps this
is not surprising; lives so cluttered, so densely materialistic, and so
overwhelmed by invasive input from our omnipresent communications technology virtually preclude noticing, let alone valuing, interior
modes of perception.

In The Stand, a flu virus, "Captain Trips" by name, kills 99.4% of the world's population, a single stroke that clears away the clatter and clutter of 20th-century technoculture and transforms America into a stage for the long-prophesied Biblical showdown between good and evil. Beneath King's elaborate plot machinations there rages another conflict, an epistemological debate precipitated by an alternation in human consciousness following the cataclysmic ravages of the superflu. The central issue of this debate—how to deal with "impossible knowledge" obtained via irrational modes of perception—becomes, in King's scenario, concrete and consequential. Indeed, it is vital to the outcome of the survivors' struggle against evil, as personified by the dark man Randall Flagg.

The Stand derives much of its power from the myth of the apocalypse, a paradigm which even in our acutely secular age "continue[s] to lie under our ways of making sense of the world" (Kermode, 28). While avoiding simplistic allegory or a schematized translation of Revelation, King taps "the power of the eschatological imagination, with its sharp contrasts between good and evil, light and darkness, with its dreams of absolute salvation and absolute degradation, and its furious denial of the established world order" (Wagar, 60). More specifically, the accidental unleashing of Captain Trips and the "fast, happy tap dance on the grave of the whole world" (Danse Macabre 440) that follows situate The Stand within various literary contexts that are relevant to its epistemological concerns.

Stephen King's Secular Eschatology

Most obviously, King's epic science-fictional saga of man-made pestilential disaster belongs with the myriad SF works that were spawned by the first secular apocalyptic narrative, Mary Shelley's The Last Man (1826); prominent on this overstuffed shelf are Jack London's 1912 novella "The Scarlet Plague," John Christopher's No Blade of Grass (1957), and George R. Stewart's Earth Abides (1949), an acknowledged influence on King's conception for The Stand (Winter, 61). This subgenre of SF, which W. Warren Wagar has charted up to 1980 in Terminal Visions (1982), remains active in such recent novels as Chelsea Quinn Yarbro's Time of the Fourth Horseman (1976), Leslie Horvitz' The Dying (1987), and Geoffrey Simmons' Pandemic (1980). But King's novel encompasses more literary territory than the sub-genre of man-made disaster novels. As Tony Magistrale has shown in Landscape of Fear (1989), King's stories in general—and The Stand in particular—belong to the American romance tradition of Hawthorne, Melville, Twain, and Poe. More precisely, it belongs to the tradition of American apocalypses which, as David Ketter, Douglas Robinson, John R. May and others have shown, extends back to the earliest days of the nation. As an imaginative response to radical cultural or historical discontinuity, "the whole question of the apocalyptic ideology, of the historical transformation of space and time from old to new, from corruption to new innocence, from death to rebirth, is fundamental to American literature" (Robinson, 3). Of course, The Stand is a product of the post-war era, a period in which "paradigms of apocalypse" (Kermode, 28) became positively ubiquitous. As Robinson and May demonstrate, American fiction from Hiroshima to the present has been dominated by works explicitly or implicitly apocalyptic; so much so that "the contemporary literary world seems genuinely to reflect a cultural climate that is itself universally apocalyptic" (May, 202).

On the surface of narrative, The Stand exhibits the three elements May identifies as "normative for traditional or classical apocalypses," (May, 24): judgment, catastrophe, and renewal—probably the shortest possible plot summary of this mammoth novel. At a deeper level, it also exhibits most of the "traditional earmarks" (Dewey, 28) of the narrower mode Joseph Dewey calls the apocalyptic temper: "a way of understanding a contemporary world by accepting the very grimmest evidence of decline and professing nevertheless a healthy conviction that history need not be consigned to simple contingency because, for the moment, questions loom too large for adequate response" (Dewey, 14).

Still, King develops his apocalyptic scenario within an insistently Christian context and loads it with Biblical allusions and references to the most influential Christian apocalyptic tract, the Revelation of John of Patmos. All this machinery links The Stand to an eschatological tradition far older than that of American apocalypses, a tradition that predates the birth of Christ (Wagar, 33—64) and thus establishes a pre-rationalist context that subtly frames its core epistemological debate.

As in the Christian apocalypse, the end of civilization in The Stand comes about because of a failure of morality: the abrogation of responsibility for technological powers inherited from two centuries of reason, science, and rationalism. Compounding the immorality of Project Blue, the government research program whose sole objective is the development of viral weapons, is the faith of its scientists and their military overlords that their control of such weapons suffices to make them invincible. Further compounding this Frankensteinian hubris is a determined denial of personal responsibility. When Stu asks Dick Dietz, one of his captors at the Stovington installation where the government is studying his immunity, precisely who is responsible for releasing the superflu, Dietz answers, "Nobody . . . On this one the responsibility spreads in so many directions that it's invisible," then remarks that "It was an accident. It could have happened any number of other ways" (104-5).

Both before and after Captain Trips comes to call, events in The Stand conform, roughly, to the four phases of traditional eschatological narrative: a period of growing evil and decay; the eruption of worldwide calamity; the end; and the arrival of a restored primal age (Wagar, 35)—although admittedly the ravages of the superflu herald the threat of an even greater calamity: the final defeat of good by "the purest evil left in the world" (503), Randall Flagg and his "rough beast of an army" (569). Reinforcing this parallel to Christian myth are the book's many references to Revelation. When, late in the novel, street-side chit-chat in Boulder turns to the subject of Flagg, one unnamed (and therefore generalized) citizen holds that "he's Satan, pure and simple."

Another avows that he's "[t]he Antichrist" and that the survivors are "living out the Book of Revelation right in our own time . . . how can you doubt it? 'And the seven vials were opened . . .' Sure sounds like the superflu to me" (888). Later still, Mother Abagail explains her unexpected departure from Boulder in a note that refers explicitly to the classic sin of Biblical eschatology: "I've sinned and presumed to know the Mind of God. My sin has been PRIDE and He wants me to find my place in His work again" (708).

All this might tempt one to shoehorn The Stand into the mold of Revelation, as Joseph Reino tries to do by arguing that all of the "ominous symbology of the Book of Revelation" is present in the novel "in spirit at least, if not as actual symbol" (Reino, 55). But to consider The Stand as little more than a map of the Christian myth of the endtime is constraining and reductive. As Magistrale argues, the novel's "elaborate allegory embracing the ultimate conflict between the forces of good and evil in the world is eventually defined in distinctly human terms . . . The Stand finally locates true religious sentiments within a secular context" (Magistrale, Landscape, 37).

The relationship of The Stand to its progenerative myth informs one of its epistemological dimension its underlying view of history. King signals that history in the world of The Stand is cyclic—not, as in Jewish and Christian eschatologies, linear (Wagar, 54)—by framing the novel with two sentences, each on a page by itself: "THE CIRCLE OPENS" (xx) and, just before the epilogue, "THE CIRCLE CLOSES" (1136). In that epilogue we learn that evil endures, that Flagg's defeat was temporary. More optimistically, the novel concludes, like many cyclic eschatologies, with a celebration of the rebirth of goodness, the death of Flagg's child, still in the womb of his mother Nadine Cross, balanced by the birth of Fran's baby and Lucy's twins, all immune to the superflu.

One of King's primary agendas in this SF epic of secular apocalypse is to critique that most potent of secularizing forces, rationalism. As Magistrale, Winter, and others have shown, in this and other novels King fires pointed sociopolitical barbs at almost every aspect of life

147

in late 20th-century America. His main target in The Stand is our faith in materialistic progress, a faith born in the early 19th-century transformation of Christian millenialism into a belief in the betterment of man through reason, science, and technology. This critique is common to the American apocalyptic tradition, most of whose texts reflect "the process of secularization that began in the nineteenth century and blossomed into the anomie of the century of unrestrained technology" (May, 32-3). And it is technology that both defines and destroys the pre-flu world.

The Waking Worlds of The Stand

If the "constantly shifting A-Prime flu" accidentally released from Project Blue incarnates the malignant potential of technology unrestrained by morality, then television and radio represent its duplicity and untrustworthiness. As channels for accurate, useful information, the media in Book I prove a dead loss. They serves only an irredeemably corrupt government trying, preposterously, to stage-manage Armageddon by withholding or distorting information about the pestilence. King deftly links this theme to the plague via the simile of Captain Trips as "chain letter" (70), a letter that communicates only death. Later, after the superflu has decimated stage-managers and viewers alike, other, non-technological, even irrational channels of communication open up, and the theme of communication becomes a focus of the novel's epistemological concerns.

For the present it is fitting that Captain Trips transforms the site of research on biological warfare, the Project Blue installation deep beneath the western California desert, from "a well-funded scientific research project" (169) into a "tomb." From his command post less than a mile away, government functionary Starkey peers through television monitors at the litter of corpses and listens through speakers to centrifuges burning out their bearings, the siren song of the engine of technology. Later, Starkey enters the installation and, through suicide, becomes one with the dead.

Elaborating the symbolic role of Project Blue is the "government plague and communicable diseases center" at Stovington, Vermont where Stu Redman is incarcerated by the increasingly desperate military. "The size of a largish metropolitan hospital" (257), Stovington is three stories of granite and marble above ground and much more beneath. Surrounded by high walls and wrought-iron fences, this labyrinth of corridors, T-junctions, offices, and labs is the very model of a modern major research facility.

Stovington means different things to different people. For the ever-rational Harold Lauder, trying to figure out where to go from Ogunquit, it acts as a magnet. For Fran Goldsmith, Harold's future traveling companion, it is the focus of her faith in authority, her need for structure. And for Nadine Cross, future bride of the dark man, it is "a symbol of sanity and rationality" (466). Locked in the strictures of pre-flu rationalism, these characters find the lure of Stovington irresistible, so their discovery that it has become "a death house" (630) is all the more shattering.

Stovington is anything but a place of "sanity and rationality." Unlike the disease control center at Atlanta where Stu is first taken for examination, the Vermont installation is run-down, slipshod, staffed not by doctors but by murderous thugs like "Dr." Elder. "The army version of a Mafia button-man" (251), Elder personifies the degradation of science and medicine. After Stu's escape and Captain Trips' final romp through the corridors of Stovington, the huge facility becomes, like Project Blue, a house of the dead. The image of the silent, deserted structure which Fran, Harold, Stu, and Glen Bateman, then Nadine, the boy Joe, and Larry Underwood find at the end of their first trek across post-flu America haunts the rest of the novel, a symbol of amoral rationalism, debased science, and corrupt technology.

As Stovington symbolizes King's technological warning—hubris clobbered by nemesis, in Brian Aldiss' witty formulation (Aldiss, 46), so does his Gothic villain personify it. Rather unsubtly, Glen Bateman, primary exponent of anti-rationalism in The Stand, describes the monstrous Flagg on three separate occasions as "the last magician of rational thought, gathering the tools of technology against us" (731, 905, 1057). And, as Magistrale has shown (Landscape, 34) King repeatedly aligns Flagg with the technology that spawned Captain Trips and the terrible "toys" that litter the decimated American landscape, "lying around, waiting to be picked up" (334).

King's figuration of "thousands of doomsday weapons" (337) as toys "like a child's set of blocks" (337), resonates throughout the novel. After a meeting of the Boulder Free Zone Committee, Nick Andros elaborates this metaphor, first pointedly alluding to Aldous Huxley's relevant dystopia, as he reflects on the "brave new world" (658) forming in Boulder:

> It was as if someone had put a large cherry bomb
> into a child's toy box. There had been a big bang and
> everything had gone everywhere. . . . Some things
> were shattered beyond repair, other things would be
> fixable, but most of the stuff had just been scattered.
> Those things were still a little too hot to handle, but
> they would be fine once they had cooled off. (658)

Ever ready to play with these technological toys is Donald Merwin Elbert—Trashcan Man to his friends—who functions in the psychological substructure of the novel as Flagg's "technological 'id'" a lunatic mirror of the Walkin Dude's pure destructive capability without his "tyrannical self-discipline" (Magistrale, Landscape, 44). Late in the novel Trash uses extrasensory powers to "sniff out" (935) a buried warhead. Seeing the radiation sign, he laughs "like a child and [claps] his hands in the stillness" (1010).

For the moment, though, most of the detritus of our technoculture is scattered, dysfunctional; the engine of technology is still, and Captain Trips has cleared space for nature. When Stu escapes from the technological tomb of Stovington, he emerges into a bucolic natural setting: "A cool evening breeze touched his face, dried the sweat on his brow. He saw with something very like wonder that there was grass, and flower beds. Night had never smelled as fragrantly sweet as this. A crescent moon rode the sky . . . He could hear the wind whispering in the pines" (257). Even Trash, high atop the Cheery Oil Company storage tanks in his home town of Powtanville, Indiana, notices that now "you could actually see Gary, because the industrial smokes that usually poured from its factory stacks were absent (280). The theme of the renewal of nature and King's many references to pastoral potency may suggest that he offers as a balm for mankind's woes some sort of small-is-beautiful back-to-nature utopia. But his stance towards science and technology in the post-flu world, which relates to the novel's debate between rationalism and irrationalism, possible and impossible knowledge, is more complex and ambiguous than this.

For the "new order" that emerges from "the destructive chaos" of Captain Trips in King's "fulfillment of the apocalyptic imagination" (Ketterer, 14) is no pastoral utopia. King avoids the extreme rejection of technology of, say, Walter J. Miller's A Canticle for Leibowitz (1959) or Russell Hoban's Ridley Walker (1980). Nor does he demonize technology as do many counterculture post-holocaust SF narratives of the '60's (Pierce, 159). Rather, through incident and dialogue, King shows that the loss of scientific, medical, and technological know-how is no blessing. As Winter observes, "[a]lthough anti-scientific, The Stand disavows scientific ignorance as the answer" (72).

The need for knowledge is a recurrent theme in Book II as the citizens of the Boulder Free Zone fret about getting their lights back on, getting heat into their homes before winter, getting their message of hope and community out beyond the boundaries of Boulder, stopping the "brain-drain" (775) of technical people to Flagg, and above all, finding a doctor. King hammers home the vulnerability of those lacking medical expertise by introducing in Chapter 46 two characters, Mark and Perion (Chapter 46), whose primary narrative function seems to be to die. Mark's appendicitis, which neither Stu nor Glen nor Fran has the slightest idea how to treat, provokes Perion to deliver King's apparent message "[Mark's] dying because we've all been spending our time learning how to bullshit each other in dorms and the

151

living rooms of cheap apartments in college towns" (531)—after which she exits the novel, dying by her own hand. But not before Mark's sickness traumatizes Fran: "There's no doctor in the house. How true it was. How horribly true. God, it was all coming at her at once, crashing down all around her. How horribly alone they were. How horribly far out on the wire they were, and somebody had forgotten the safety net" (519). Mark's death anticipates the crisis Fran may have to face delivering her baby if a doctor doesn't wander in to Boulder. (Later, Dr. George Richardson obligingly shows up.)

Technical as well as medical knowledge is urgently needed if the nascent Boulder community is to survive. In one of many conversations with Stu, Glen admits, somewhat reluctantly, that a "necessary requirement" for "enlightened, democratic communities . . . in the 1990's and early 2000's" is "enough technical people . . . to get the lights back on," and that "[i]n the post-flu world, technological know-how is going to replace gold as the most perfect medium of exchange" (332).

But if King's "new order" is no pastoral utopia, neither is it a technological utopia like that envisioned by, say, George Allan England in The Afterglow (1911), the final novel of his Darkness and Dawn trilogy. For England, technologically based civilization is an absolute exigency for human fulfillment, the best hope of the race; for King, it's at best a dangerous necessity. Throughout The Stand, characters articulate and events reinforce King's strong reservations about technology as a basis for society.

Of course, technology is the manifestation of rationalism, the primary philosophy underlying 20th-century technoculture. And embedded in the rationalist tradition are a cluster of epistemological assumptions about our ability to comprehend our state of existence, about the limits of perceptions, and about accessibility to humans of knowledge about their state of being, about perception, and about how best to order our society—assumptions which the events of The Stand persistently call into question. Not surprisingly, it is self-avowed "Luddite" (336) Glen, again lecturing Stu, who links Captain Trips, rationalism, and technology:

"The superflu we can charge off to the stupidity of the human race. It doesn't matter if we did it or the Russians, or the Latvians. Who emptied the beaker loses importance beside the general truth: At the end of all rationalism, the mass grave. The laws of physics, the laws of biology, the axioms of mathematics, they're all part of the deathtrip, because we are what we are. If it hadn't been Captain Trips, it would have been something else. The fashion was to blame it on 'technology,' but 'technology' is the trunk of the tree, not the roots. The roots are rationalism, and I would define that word so: 'Rationalism is the idea we can ever understand anything about the state of being.' It is a deathtrip. It always has been. So you can charge the superflu off to rationalism if you want." (730)

Significantly, while Glen challenges the entire post-Enlightenment thrust towards progress through rationalism, he does not argue that knowledge or even science is inherently evil, but rather that the fault lies in what we do with that knowledge, in human nature, in "what we are."

The antithesis of rationalism is irrationalism, and Glen interprets the coming to Boulder of so many survivors under the "flat of powers we don't understand" (730) as a sign of the power of irrational, supernatural forces in the post-flu world. This, in turn, signals that "the age of rationalism has passed," as "it almost [did] in the 1960's, the so-called Age of Aquarius, and . . . during the Middle Ages" (730). Now, with the "bright dazzle" of technology gone from his eyes, man can finally see "dark magic . . . A universe of marvels where water flows uphill and trolls live in the deepest woods and dragons live under the mountains. Bright wonders, white power. 'Lazarus, come forth.' Water into wine. And . . . and just maybe . . . the casting out of devils . . . The lifetrip" (731). The mix of allusions from the Bible and secular fantasy links Glen's flight of fancy to the novel's eschatological context even as it hints that maybe he's flown a bit far beyond the sensible bounds of speculation. In any case, for Glen this development heralds a, major evolutionary advance in the human species, a far-reaching transformation of consciousness itself: "we may be beginning to accept—only subconsciously now, and with plenty of slips backward due to culture lag—a different definition of existence. The idea that we can never understand anything about the state of being. And if rationalism is a deathtrip, then irrationalism might very well be a lifetrip . . . at least until it proves otherwise" (730).

The immediate manifestations of this transformation are the many forms of heightened (irrational) perception—dreams, telepathy, prophetic blackouts, hypnotic trances, communication with the dead—which, especially in Book II, provide the characters with "impossible" knowledge and in so doing pose the immediate problem of what to do with it. How much credence and seriousness can one give to information and directives received from irrational sources? No mere philosophical abstraction, this question becomes exigent as good and evil line up for their imminent confrontation. So while The Stand is not solely an epistemological novel, it does raise broad epistemological concerns that become vital to its resolution: How do we know what we know? How does the mode of apprehension of knowledge influence our attitude towards it? That is, how should we interpret and act upon knowledge obtained via a medium whose very existence confounds our assumptions and beliefs?

These issues come to the fore late in the novel when Fran must decide how to deal with her intuitive, "impossible" awareness of the danger in the house where she and the rest of the Boulder Free Zone committee are meeting: "All of a sudden she didn't want to be in this house . . . She wanted to get out. In fact, she wanted them all to get out" (872). The danger is quite real; although Fran doesn't know it, Harold Lauder has made a bomb which Nadine has planted in a nearby closet. But, locked in "culture lag," Fran dithers disastrously. Since "[t]here [is] no reason for the feeling," she dismisses it:

> She was frightened—and frightened of her own baseless fear, if such a thing were possible. Where had this stifling, claustrophobic feeling come from? She knew that what you were supposed to do with baseless feelings was to ignore them . . . at least in the old world. But what about Tom Cullen's trance? What about Leo Rockway?
> Get out of here, the voice inside suddenly cried. Get them all out!
> But it was so crazy. She shifted again and decided to say nothing. (874)

Later Stu and Nick also sense the danger. But it is too late. Harold detonates the bomb. Twenty people are wounded. Seven die.

This incident anticipates a similar but even more urgent decision, one which shapes the climax of The Stand. On her deathbed, Mother Abagail presents Glen, Ralph, Larry, and Stu with instructions she claims to have received from God: they are to walk from Boulder to Las Vegas without food, water, transport, or protection—with nothing, in fact, except "the clothes [they] stand up in" (904)—there to face Flagg. What the four men make of this irrational directive becomes one fulcrum upon which the novel's resolution turns.

The emphasis this device gives to irrationalism in the primary narrative of The Stand may suggest that the novel advocates the wholesale abandonment of rationalism. But King eschews this simple stance just as he disavows complete rejection of technology. To be sure, as Reino and others have observed, many of King's novels betray a distinctly anti-rationalist bias. But The Stand offers more than mere "anti-rationalist outbursts" (Reino, 53); through his hero Stu Redman and an important minor character, King balances Glen's vision of a coming millennium of irrationalism and dark magic. Repeatedly, King pairs Stu with Glen in conversation. Responding to Glen's rosy view of irrationalism as lifetrip, Stu admits that he is superstitious but rejects the prospect of living "with no science . . . worshipping the sun, maybe . . . thinking monsters are rolling bowling balls across the sky when it thunders . . . Why, it seems like a kind of slavery to me" (730).

To develop this counterpoint, King introduces Judge Farris, a citizen of Boulder whose primary narrative function is to become an early sacrifice to Flagg. But in the novel's epistemological debate, Judge Farris serves as the exponent of man's need for rationalism. When Larry visits the Judge to ask him to go to Las Vegas to spy on Flagg, their conversation turns to Mother Abagail, who has just unexpectedly left the Free Zone for the surrounding wilderness. To the Judge, the departure of this "amazing woman" who is "completely outside any rational frame of reference" (796) may not be such a bad thing: "Maybe," he tells Larry, "people should be free to judge for themselves what the lights in the sky are, and if one tree has a face or if the face was only a trick of the light and shadow" (796).

Larry is confused, so the Judge elaborates. In terms that recall Glen's new world of "dark magic," he wonders whether "we need to reinvent that whole tiresome business of gods and saviors and ever-afters before we reinvent the flushing toilet . . . I wonder if this is the right time for gods." Avowedly "a rational old curmudgeon," the Judge articulates a response to the irrational, which may ring true to many readers, loaded with Biblical references:

> "None of us want to see portents and omens, no matter how much we like our ghost stories and the spooky films. None of us want to really see a Star in the East or a pillar of fire by night. We want peace and rationality and routine. If we have to see God in the black face of an old woman, it's bound to remind us that there's a devil for every god—and our devil may be closer than we like to think." (796)

156

In such conversations, major and minor characters alike return again and again to the cluster of issues that swirl about the rationalism/irrationalism axis of King's novel. The pestilential decimation of the pre-flu world foregrounds these issues, and the survivors' discussions in the post-flu world elaborate them. But these worlds are only two of the landscapes of King's "long tale of dark Christianity" (xv). The third world of The Stand, a world where irrational forces and dark magic hold sway and where the novel's epistemological issues assume new dimensions, is the world of dream.

Stephen King's Post-apocalyptic Dream World

> Dreams are like life, only more so.
> —G. K. Chesterton

Once Captain Trips has rendered science and technology all but impotent, dreams return in force dreams of a primitive, supernatural kind. King's use of this literary device differs strikingly from that of most modern writers. In the modern and post-modern novel, dreams are usually psychologically or somatically based and function primarily to reveal facets of character or context not available through action or dialogue. But in The Stand, dreams are minatory, premonitory, and prophetic. These literary functions date back to Dante's The Divine Comedy (ca. 1320), to the Bible, and to pre-Biblical epics such as The Illiad (ca. 8th century BC) and The Aeneid (19 BC).

As in these early epics, dreams in The Stand come from an external supernatural agent—perhaps, as Mother Abagail would have it, from God. They are explicit and realistic, and require little interpretation by characters or readers. They communicate directives and information to the dreamers, who must then figure out what to do with the "impossible" knowledge thus received. While not the only irrational mode of perception in The Stand, dreams are the most powerful and pervasive. In fact, the trajectory of Book I, in which the survivors of Captain Trips wander across the depopulated American continent on their way to either Boulder or Las Vegas, is governed by dreams.

These characters experience two opposing dreams—one of Mother Abagail and a Nebraska cornfield, the other of pursuit by "the man with no face" Randall Flagg. So omnipresent are these dreams as to constitute another world coexistent with the American wasteland.

King introduces these dreams gradually, making clear from the outset that they are not rationally explicable. Before anyone realizes their commonalty, he signals this feature by having the dreamers use common phrases and images, even when recounting their initial dreams, which have little detail. Stu's dream in Stovington is vague: he sees a cornfield, hears guitar music, and senses something evil in the corn. But his thoughts about it introduce Flagg's signature phrase, "the man with no face" (106), which will recur in other accounts, and the image of the weasel, which will reappear in Chapter 45 when Flagg supernaturally attacks Mother Abagail in the waking world. In a proximate dream, Nick Andros, still in Shoyo, Arkansas, sees a cornfleld redolent with "[a] sense of home" (192). Sensing "something in the corn . . . watching him," he thinks "Ma, weasel's got in the henhouse!'"(192).

These dreams are not merely monitory; they are an active principle, a "force . . . too powerful to be denied" (621). In his first dream, Stu feels the imperative of the cornfield: "This is where I ought to get to, Stu thought dimly. Yeah, this is the place, all right" (106). In Shoyo, Nick feels "an inner urge to hurry, something so strong yet indefinable that it amounted to a subconscious command" (385). Later, on the road from Vermont to Nebraska, Stu dreams that Mother Abagail is urging him to "move em along faster still, Stuart" (557).

In addition to moving the plot along, these opposing dreams function in other ways. In Chapter 40, for example, Nick experiences a dual dream. He first dreams of perching on a precipice, the desert "spread out below him like a relief map" (360), and of being tempted by Flagg, who in a sibilant whisper offers "Everything you see will be yours if you fall down on your knees and worship me." Nick refuses, and this dream segues into a recurrence of the cornfield dream—but in far greater detail than elsewhere in the novel. He hears Mother Abagail playing the guitar and singing a hymn, learns the precise location of her home "Polk County, Nebraska, west of Omaha and a little north of Osceola" (362)—and hears her invitation to "come see me anytime, boy, and bring your friends" (363).

Eschewing ambiguity, King grounds Nick's dream in psychological credibility—Flagg tempts him with the very thing a deaf mute would likely want most, the ability to speak and hear—and layers it with dense realistic detail: the desert landscape Nick sees from the precipice, the sounds he hears in both dreams particulars of the cornfield, Mother Abagail's appearance, her shack, etc. (361 ff). King also uses the dream to deepen Nick's characterization (his refusal of Flagg's offer) and to enhance the terrifying perception of the novel's monstrous villain. The thing that tempts Nick is "not a man but the shape of a man. As if the figure had been cut from the fabric of reality and what really stood beside him was a negative man, a black hole in the shape of a man" (360). And the second part of Nick's dream gives us information about Mother Abagail, prior to her introduction into the narrative proper in Chap. 45, and advances the narrative with her invitation to Nick, which leads to his departure from Shoyo in Chap. 43.

More subtly, Nick's dream operates within the novel's structure of religious allusions. Its first part extends the book's Biblical references via the (rather heavy-handed) parallel to the temptation of Christ and suggests the identifications of Nick with Christ and Flagg with Satan. And its second part alludes to the Bible through the Edenic imagery in the hymn Nick hears Mother Abagail singing ("I come to the garden alone . . . ") (362). The conjunction of the two dreams, which "blend together . . . with hardly a seam to show the difference" (361), suggests that it may be Nick's refusal of Flagg's temptation that admits him to Mother Abagail's "garden"—less literally, to a place in the dream world (a state of mind) where he can communicate with her in spite of his physical handicaps.

More allusive and realistic than symbolic or allegorical, Nick's dream illustrates the admixture of elements, often exaggerated or distorted by the dreamer's neuroses and fears, in most dreams in Books

I and II of The Stand. It also develops the theme of communication via the notion of (irrational) communication in the dream world. While this world does not penetrate the waking world in King's novel as it does in, say, Ramsey Campbell's Incarnate (1983), it is linked to that world by the transfer of information. Nick's handicap highlights the extraordinary character of this transmission: "Unlike all the other dreams he had in his life, Nick did not have to lip-read these. He could actually hear what people were saying" (360-1).

The most extreme instance of impossible communication in the dreamworld transcends the barrier of death. Late in the novel, after Tom Cullen has left Flagg's encampment to return on foot to Boulder, he falls asleep beside the highway outside Las Vegas. In a dream, he hears Nick warn him that Flagg knows about him and direct him to "keep going east" and to "look for God's Finger" (997). Later Nick further directs him northeast towards "a huge granite dome" (1103), and, later still, instructs him in the care of injured Stu Redman. Although Tom knows Nick is mute, he unquestioningly accepts what Nick tells him, thinking that, after all, "dreams were funny things, anything could happen in a dream, and in Tom's, Nick had been talking" (997). What Tom does not know is that Nick is dead, a victim of the bomb Nadine has planted in Stu and Fran's house.

Dreams like Tom's, which come late in The Stand, are particularized by the exigencies of King's complicated plot. But the shared dreams of Book I serve character delineation as well as plot advancement. The least individuated are the dreams of the cornfield and Mother Abagail; these are dominated by bucolic images of fertility and haunted by fear of something evil in the corn. The pursuit dreams, on the other hand, are personalized by the neuroses, fears, and waking concerns of the dreamers. Fran dreams of going upstairs to bury her recently deceased father and finding under the sheet "[s]omething—someone—filled with dark life and hideous good cheer" (248) holding "a twisted coat hanger," a gift for her unborn child. Stu dreams of "a cold black shadow where his face should have been" blocking his escape from the "echoing tomb" (337) of Stovington. And Larry dreams of being chased through the Lincoln tunnel by "a black man ... worse than the walking dead" (416) and, later, of Flagg bearing in his arms the decaying body of Rita Blakemore, "now stiff and swollen, the flesh ripped by woodchucks and weasels." These dreams are thus empowered by Fran's maternal anxiety, Stu's phobia of incarceration, and Larry's guilt over Rita's death.

Most dreams in The Stand are both premonitory and prophetic. Glen considers them "a constructive force, in spite of their ability to frighten" (538), remarking that they "seem to presage some future struggle" and provide "cloudy pictures of a protagonist ... and an antagonist. An adversary, if you like" (538). Later, Harold dreams prophetically of "dying halfway down a steep grade of tumbled rocks and moonscape boulders" (562), a dream that anticipates his betrayal by Flagg, whose "frightful red Eye" beckons him westward across the Rockies. But the main recipient of prophetic dreams is Mother Abagail. "Prophecy," she tells a newly arrived group of supplicants at her Nebraska home, "is the gift of God and everyone has a smidge of it" (502). For her, dreams are a pipeline to God. After all, she thinks, "God did speak to folks; hadn't He talked to Noah about the ark, telling him how many cubits long and how many deep and how many wide? Yes. And she believed He had spoken to her as well, not from a burning bush or out of a pillar of fire, but in a still small voice" (476).

God's voice tells Mother Abagail many things. It tells her to eschew dependence on technology. On her hundredth birthday, when offered a tap into the city water supply, she refuses, just as earlier she had refused a "kind offer of a flushing toilet" (476), because the "still small voice" of God said "Abby, you are going to need your hand-pump. You enjoy your lectricity all you want, Abby, but you keep those oil-lamps of yours full and keep the wicks trimmed" (476). The voice also details her mission, in dreams that begin two years before the outbreak of the superflu: "In my dreams I saw myself going west ... until I could see the Rocky Mountains." The information the voice provides is quite specific: she sees "signs ... no, not signs from God but regular road signs, and every one of them saying things like BOULDER, COLORADO, 609 MILES or THIS WAY TO BOULDER" (502).

With the formation of the Boulder Free Zone, the shared dreams stop. But Mother Abagail's prophetic dreams continue. Before leaving Boulder, she reflects on the future of the Free Zone: "They would get the power back on, of course. It was one of the things God had shown her in her dreams. She knew a goodish number of things about what was to come here—some from the dreams, some from her own common sense. The two were too intertwined to tell apart." (640). Much later she obtains from her dreams the ultimate "impossible knowledge," the time of her own death. After visiting her sick-bed, Larry tells Fran and Stu that she "told [him] the Lord was going to take her home at the sunrise" (900). And so He does.

In stark contrast to Mother Abagail, some characters adamantly reject their dreams. Harold Lauder, ever the rationalist, wants to suppress his dreams with the drug Veronal. Even more extreme is the denial by a character whose continuous, vivid dreams afford her information unavailable even to Mother Abagail. Nadine Cross becomes almost frantic when, early in her trek westward, she learns that her companions Larry, Lucy Swann, and the primitive boy "Joe" share the pursuit dream. Striving to relate the mystical to the technological, Lucy wonders "Is somebody using a ray on us?" (464) But Nadine will have none of it: "'I don't dream!,' she cried sharply, almost hysterically" (465). Later, during an argument about where to go after their dead-end visit to Stovington, Nadine agrees to accompany them to Nebraska—but not for irrational reasons. Avowing that she would rather "place her faith in radios, not visions," (621), she rejects the dream directive: "As long as there was some rational basis for pushing on to Nebraska, ... fine. But she wanted it understood that she wasn't going along on the basis of a lot of metaphysical bullshit." Like other conversations in Book I, this dialogue highlights the limitations of rationality, its inability to encompass experience in the postflu world.

In fact, Nadine has been dreaming all along, profusely and richly—but not of Nebraska—and through her dreams, King clarifies her special place in the epistemological matrix of The Stand. In contrast to the others' opposing dreams of Flagg and Mother Abagail, Nadine dreams "[o]nly of the dark man" (631). And in those dreams she acquires detailed knowledge about the dark man which others cannot access: that his name is Randall Flagg, that his opponents "had either been crucified or driven mad somehow and set free to wander in the boiling sink of Death Valley" (631), and that "small groups of technical people" were moving to Las Vegas, "where the main concentration of people was growing" (631). Of all the characters in Boulder only Tom Cullen, the only dreamer to see Flagg's face, is similarly privileged in the communications net of the novel's dreamworld.

Nadine's experiences generalize the theme of irrational communication to modes other than dreams. Sitting in the Sunrise Amphitheater near the summit of Flagstaff Mountain outside Boulder, she feels Flagg's presence across the Rockies, and, using a planchette, "a triangular spider on three stubby legs, pencil pointing down," (765) communicates with her future husband. At which point we learn that just as Mother Abagail's communication link to God predates the coming of Captain Trips, so does Nadine's to Flagg, a development which introduces into the novel an unnerving element of predestination. More than a dozen years earlier, while still in college, Nadine joined some girls playing with a planchette, trying to receive "messages from the astral plane" (765). But when Nadine plays, the game turns deadly serious. In "big, slanting capital letters that slashed across the white page" (769), Flagg greets his bride-to-be:

NADINE, NADINE, NADINE, the whirling
planchette wrote. HOW I LOVE NADINE TO
BE MY TO LOVE MY NADINE TO BE MY
QUEEN . . . YOU ARE DEAD WITH THE

REST OF THEM YOU ARE IN THE
DEADBOOK WITH THE REST OF THEM . . .
THE WORLD THE WORLD SOON THE
WORLD IS DEAD AND . . . WE ARE IN THE
HOUSE OF THE DEAD NADINE. (769-770)

But Nadine doesn't need a planchette to foresee Flagg's fall. In his lair high above Las Vegas, she confronts her monstrous husband. Looking "like some pallid deranged sibyl" (1001) she prophesies the arrival of the four men who are at that moment trekking westward from Boulder: "They're coming. Stu Redman, Glen Bateman, Ralph Brentner, and Larry Underwood. They're coming and they'll kill you like a chicken-stealing weasel." She also foretells the dissolution and ultimate destruction of his empire:

> "The effective half-life of evil is always rela-
> tively short. People are whispering about you . . .
> They're saying your weapons expert has gone crazy
> and you didn't know it was going to happen. They're
> afraid that what he brings back from the desert next
> time may be for them instead of for the people in the
> East. And they're leaving."
> Her eyes gazed blankly over his shoulder to the
> east. "I see them," she whispered. They're leaving
> their posts in the dead of night, and your Eye doesn't
> see them." (1001-2)

Nadine's use of the metaphor of half-life, drawn from radiation physics, in the context of her reference to Flagg's "weapons expert" carries a heavy ironic weight to readers aware of what Trashcan Man has found in the nearby desert.

Trash, too, has special gifts of perception. Long before his slide into total madness, he receives Flagg's summons in a dream: "come to my city . . . West. Beyond the mountains" (570). In the city "Cibola, Seven-in-One, the City that is Promised" (571), a reference to the fabled city of Indian and Hispanic legend, Trash becomes Flagg's "idiot savant" (936). As Lloyd Henried tells Danya Jurgens, Trash can find a weapon by just "sniff[ing] it out" (935). Lloyd's explanation of Trash's wild talent reiterates the novel's dominant metaphor for nuclear weapons even as it foreshadows its climax: "It isn't really so strange. Most of western Nevada and eastern California was owned by the good old U. S. A. It's where they tested their toys, all the way up to A bombs. He'll be dragging one of those back someday" (935). Sure enough, as Trash wanders "the devil's frying pan" (1004), he functions "like an infrared scope that senses heat in the darkness and reveals those heat sources as vague red devil shapes" (1008)—a passage whose particularly deft similes link Flagg, Trash, technology, and the implements of modern war to evil.

Trash's boss is the only character in The Stand who obtains "impossible knowledge" primarily via a device. Flagg certainly "[has] a way of knowing things" (917). He knows that his counterparts in Boulder have sent Judge Farris, Danya Jurgens, and one other to spy on him. He knows that Brad Kitchner has fixed a power outage in Boulder. He knows about Mother Abagail's return to Boulder from the wilderness and about her death. All this knowledge he obtains with "a sort of third eye" (967), a magical device which Joseph Reino has identified with the "Wedjet" of ancient Egyptian mythology (Reino, 59). Flagg no more understands this ability than his counterparts across the Rockies understand their heightened perceptions; but he certainly doesn't argue about it: "It was like [his] levitating ability; something he had and accepted but which he didn't really understand" (967).

Like Mother Abagail, Flagg is not omnipotent. Sometimes his Eye falls "mysteriously blind" (967). He doesn't know the particulars of Mother Abagail's death-bed instructions to Stu, Glen, Ralph, Larry, and Fran. He doesn't know that Danya will kill herself. He doesn't know that Trashcan Man will blow up his aircraft and haul back from the desert a warhead that will destroy Las Vegas. In The Stand as in Christian myth, perfect knowledge is available only to the Lord, and, as Nadine reflects, whatever Flagg may be, "God, he's not" (971).

Another thing Flagg's Eye can't see is Tom Cullen. Tom, the pure innocent, antithesis of the dark man, belongs to the literary tradition "of the sainted idiot, whose purity of soul provides him with a direct conduit to God" (Magistrale, Moral Voyages, 70). Intellectually a child, Tom's mental retardation limits his rational perception. But beneath his surface enfeeblement, he has powers that range far beyond rationality, powers that emerge during his blackouts and under hypnosis. In dreams, Tom alone sees the face of Flagg, the face of everyman that masks the face of the demon:

> "He looks like anybody you see on the street.
> But when he grins, birds fall dead off telephone
> lines. When he looks at you a certain way, your
> prostate goes bad and your urine burns. The grass
> yellows up and dies where he spits. He's always
> outside. He came out of time. He doesn't know
> himself. He has the name of a thousand demons.
> Jesus knocked him into a herd of pigs once. His
> name is Legion. He's afraid of us. We're inside.
> He knows magic. He can call the wolves and live
> in the crows. He's the king of nowhere." (806)

The Biblical allusions in this powerful description, which again link Flagg to traditional apocalyptic myth, are of a piece with Tom's gift of prophecy; no longer Nick's enfeebled traveling companion, he is now "more than that Tom," he is "God's Tom" (807).

The whole elaborate substructure of irrational and extrasensory powers various characters develop throughout The Stand—the shared dreams, Mother Abagail's God-given directives, Flagg's almost-allseeing Eye, Tom's hypnotic prophecies suggest that Glen Bateman may have been right when he suggested that he and the other survivors are becoming aware of "a different definition of existence," a result of some mystical or metaphysical transformation of consciousness. The theme of heightened perception, as Winter notes, is supported by the complex narrative structure of the novel, which "begins with a disjointed multiple viewpoint technique that subtly collapses inward until even the consciousness of the characters is interwoven in the book's final pages" (Winter, 71).

Perhaps the most striking incarnation of this theme is "Joe," the primitive child originally in Nadine's care whom Larry adopts as surrogate son. In the field of Larry's love, Joe emerges from his solipsistic state to regain his identity as Leo Rockway. But he retains his extrasensory abilities. Leo is instinctively afraid of Harold, refuses to enter his house, and sees through his elaborately constructed facade: "He smiles a lot," Leo tells Larry. "But I think there might be worms inside him, making him smile. Big white worms eating up his brain" (683). Staggered by this insight, Larry tries to communicate with Leo telepathically, succeeds, and finds that he possess a wealth of "impossible knowledge" one of which requires immediate action. Leo knows that Nadine and Harold have left Boulder to join Flagg, that before leaving they planted a deadly device in Stu and Fran's house, and that Harold inscribed his hate and his schemes in the diary Fran almost found when she broke into his house: "It's all written down! You know! Frannie knows! Talk to Frannie!" (845). When Larry responds by mentioning the Committee, Leo becomes almost frantic, for he knows that the parameters of existence have changed "Not the committee! The committee won't help you, it won't help anyone, the committee is the old way, he laughs at your committee because it's the old way and the old ways are his ways, you know, Fran knows, if you talk together you can—" (845).

Through Larry's thoughts and comments about Leo's trances, King emphasizes that whatever change in perception has taken place isn't limited to childlike primitives, retarded intuitives, and demented paranoiacs. To Stu Larry says, "Leo kind of sees into people. He's not the only one, either. Maybe there were always people like that, but there seems to be a little bit more of it around since the flu" (692). And, reflecting on one of those trances, he ruminates that "[Leo] wasn't the only one; how many times in the few days he had been here [in Boulder] had Larry seen someone just stop dead on the street, looking blankly at nothing for a moment, and then go on. Things had changed. The whole range of human perception seemed to have stepped up a notch" (683).

A World of Choice

> I have set before you life and death, the blessing
> and the curse; therefore choose life, that both you and
> your descendants may live.
> —Deuteronomy

But if everyone is acting under directives obtained via irrational modes of perception and basing decisions almost entirely on impossible knowledge from some supernatural, mystical, or metaphysical source, it would be tempting to see this whole vast scenario as predestinate, a heavy deistic hand first eliminating most of the world's peoples, then moving around the rest like chessmen to set up a long-prophesied showdown in Las Vegas. And so the novel's epistemological issues merge with its broader theme of free will. But however heavy King's hand may be, it is clear that his characters do have options. Even the shared dreams, Glen notes, offer choice not compulsion: "We're being given the means to help shape our own futures, perhaps. A kind of fourth-dimensional free-will: the chance to choose in advance of events" (538).

Much later, when Mother Abagail tells Stu, Glen, Larry, and Ralph to abandon rationality, trust in the Lord, and walk to Las Vegas to make their stand against Flagg, she makes the point: "God don't lay no bribes. He just makes a sign and lets people take it as they will" (904). As the four men and Fran try to decide whether to believe Mother Abagail that God brought them together in Boulder only "to send [them] further, on a quest ... to try and destroy this Dark Prince, this Man of Far Leagues" (904) and whether to obey her directive, she reiterates that "[t]here's always a choice. That's God's way, always will be. Your will is still free. Do as you will. There's no set of leg-irons on you" (905).

Through Mother Abagail's final speech, King links the theme of free will to the novel's eschatological context and its anti-technological warning:

> "I sinned in pride. So have you all, all sinned in pride. Ain't you heard it said, put not your faith in the lords and princes of this world? . . . Electric lights ain't the answer, Stu Redman. CB radio ain't either, Ralph Brentner. Sociology won't end it, Glen Bateman. . . . The bad moon has risen. You propose nothing in the sight of God." (902)

Although the sacrificial deaths of Glen, Stu, Larry, and Ralph are final, Flagg's defeat is not, and The Stand ends where it began. The circle of King's vast novel closes on a world where good will surely again have to face down evil. For the moment, though, the post-flu world is free of the oppressive clutter of technology. And apparently those still alive have entered a new definition of existence precipitated by a transformation of consciousness which, the novel suggests, has restored the balance between the rational and the irrational that in the pre-flu world was seriously skewed. What endures beyond the cataclysmic end of civilization, the heightening of human perception, and the fiery purification of Flagg's society of techies in Las Vegas are free will and the moral imperatives of responsibility to self and community. In these constants King offers hope, however faint, that the incurably social and technological human animal may finally learn to temper his need for technology with a degree of moral responsibility the absence of which allowed those in the pre-flu world—our world—to produce the plague that begins the novel and the bomb that ends it.

169

WORKS CITED

Aldiss, Brian. Trillion Year Spree: The History of Science Fiction. New York: Atheneum, 1986.

Dewey, Joseph. In a Dark Time: The Apocalyptic Temper in the American Novel of the Nuclear Age. West Lafayette, IN: Purdue University Press, 1990.

Frye, Northrup. Anatomy of Criticism: Four Essays. New York: Atheneum, 1968.

Hoppenstand, Gary and Ray B. Browne, eds. The Gothic World of Stephen King: Landscape of Nightmares. Bowling Green, OH: Bowling Green University Popular Press, 1987.

Kermode, Frank. The Sense of an Ending: Studies in the Theory of Fiction. New York: Oxford University Press, 1967.

Ketterer, David. New Worlds for Old: The Apocalyptic Imagination, Science Fiction, and American Literature. Garden City, N.Y.: Doubleday, 1974.

King, Stephen. Danse Macabre. New York: Everest House, 1981; Berkley 1982, rev..

King, Stephen. The Stand: The Complete and Uncut Edition. New York: Signet, 1991.

Magistrale, Anthony S. The Moral Voyages of Stephen King. Mercer Island, WA: Starmont House, 1989.

Magistrale, Anthony S. Landscape of Fear: Stephen King's American Gothic. Bowling Green, OH: Bowling Green University Popular Press, 1988.

May, John R. Toward a New Earth: Apocalypse in the American Novel. Notre Dame, IN: University of Notre Dame Press, 1972.

Pierce, John R. Great Themes of Science Fiction. Westport, CT: Greenwood Press, 1987.

Reino, Joseph. Stephen King: The First Decade, Carrie to Pet Sematary. Boston, MA: Twayne, 1988.

Robinson, Douglas. American Apocalypses: The Image of the End of the World in American Literature. Baltimore, MD: Johns Hopkins University Press, 1985.

Saltzman, Arthur M. Designs of Darkness in Contemporary American Fiction. Philadelphia, PA: University of Pennsylvania Press, 1990.

Wagar, W. Warren. Terminal Visions: The Literature of Last Things. Bloomington, IN: Indiana University Press, 1982.

Winter, Douglas E. Stephen King: The Art of Darkness. New York: New American Library: 1984, Signet: 1986, rev..

Zamora, Lois Parkinson, ed. The Apocalyptic Vision in America: Interdisciplinary Essays on Myth and Culture. Bowling Green, OH: Bowling Green University Popular Press, 1982.

CHAPTER NINE

Dialogue Within the Archetypal
Community of The Stand

Ed Casebeer

There's no God, only an eye here and there
that sees clearly.
Charles Simic, The World Doesn't End

Such a novel as Stephen King's The Stand complicates classical
narrative analysis, e.g. a conflict plot in which protagonist and antagonist develop their relationship in the ascending and descending intensity of complication, rising action, climax, falling action, and resolution. If Flagg is the antagonist, who is the protagonist? Stu, Larry, Tom,
the Free Zone, humanity, God? I will address the issue, perhaps by
bypassing it, with tactics synthesizing the methods of Mikhail Bakhtin
and the psychoanalytical theory of the post-Jungian, James Hillman;
Bakhtin gives me a strategy for responding to an unresolved
heteroglossic novel such as The Stand while Hillman provides me a
useful cognitive model: the psyche as a community of archetypal personae.

My synthesis leads me to consider the novel as an analog of the
human psyche: the text is an unfinalized process which has been enacted by the writer and is to be enacted by the reader through the communal psyche enabled within each by such enactment of the text's
characters, plot, and setting. Although his own necessary dialogue with
a materialistic dialectic blocks some paths between his approach and
Hillman's Jungian idealism, Bakhtin anticipated and extended into
narrative theory much of the same perspective. Hillman's locus of
"reality" is more internal than Bakhtin's, at the interface where the
diurnal and material connect with psychological, and is more pure
process, more evanescent, more tentative, a more inviting environment

for the multiplicity which promotes the dialogue which Bakhtin recommends. Yet both of them emphasize the community and its internal ecological processes rather than isolating such individual phenomena as the protagonist or the ego. Like Hillman, Bakhtin emphasizes contiguity rather than unity. In fact, the discourse that each initiates in such texts as The Dialogic Imagination and Revisioning Psychology irritates and confounds the rational reader expecting sequence and conclusion: like Norman Brown in Love's Body, both thinkers proceed analogically rather than logically, often through discrete passages in juxtaposition, radiating psychologically as well as intellectually, continually presenting rather than concluding, proposing new questions in answer to questions. Thus, rather than trying to ascertain unity by archaeologically exploring a text, emphasizing fixed perspective, structure, mechanical system, inevitable chronological sequence, linearity, goal, and resolution, Bakhtin attends to the ecological processes of the text as it is being read, the heterogeneous perspective (heteroglossia) and the decentralization of narrator and protagonist (carnival) dialogue, dynamic, serendipitous spatial juxtaposition, radiation into unfinished process—a non-Aristotelian theory for the finished creations of the right brain, for comedy, for fantasy. Thus, he de-emphasizes the Casebeer dynamics of moving a protagonist through a conflicted plot structure. Applying his approach to The Stand, we can see the protagonist constellated among several archetypal figures. As Hillman suggests, these figures are manifestations of archetypal processes within the psyche.

Plot and setting combining with character, such a novel is a mirror of its author's psyche, held now as a mirror before its reader's. The terms that provide such continuity, nexus, template for the dyad thus linked by the text are archetypal: King's success with one of the largest audiences ever assembled by a writer is evidence of his fidelity to such universals as he apprehends; his much acclaimed realistic technique may be actually texturing of the archetypal with local detail as he has suggested, incidentally in two recent interviews:

[Characters] should have enough texture to feel real, not slick or oily. You have to like them a lot . . . (McCullaugh, 54)

This gets real close to why a lot of the books have worked . . . because I'm not afraid to go back and do the same old shit time after time, if I feel like I can texture the story enough to warrant that repetition . . . It's better to say let it happen, this is the classic way for it to happen, we textured and layered the story enough. (Wood, 26)

"Texturing" is King's contemporary brand-name detail, microscopic zoom, the precise phoneme, a turn of phrase, a smell, and a host of other minutiae which he brings to layer the archetype through his and our sensoria until it is dressed in our images, voices our sounds, pushes carts in our supermarkets beside us. We access such an archetype within ourselves (where a community of archetypes always resides, awaiting the call of history) by mistaking it in its ephemeral dress for one of us. Or perhaps that is what we in fact are: archetypes layered and textured by our daily histories. Or perhaps our histories texture us, place expressions on our faces. That his works accommodate so many readers suggests the opposing but related conclusions that I am linking in this essay: while Hillman might argue that King's success lies in his tapping a shared cultural consciousness, Bakhtin's attention to figures other than protagonist and antagonist suggests that the resultantly unfinalized novel accommodates the individual vision. For me, the concept of the textured archetype bridges the oppositions here. King's novels accommodate both the general and the particular: the general by universality of character and situation, the particular and a resistance to a structural closure that allows individual closure to occur, e.g. Flagg's resurrection in the uncut Stand. But the texturing of archetype allows him to remain faithful to "the same old shit" and, through a degree of individuation, yet seduce the reader into making the personal closures that allow her to claim the text.

175

In the following, I will limit myself to the constellated archetypal characters, but I remain aware of other Bakhtinian dialogues that I may conduct by bringing into juxtaposition other levels of character and setting, canon and genre. But before I begin, I want to juxtapose character to point of view since that is omniscient and character enters either as a result of its focus or, more frequently, its modulation into the voice of the kind of character which I will call "archetypal." King has expressed his theory on narrator in Danse Macabre: he sees the narrator as mediating for us the text by beholding its events as an "agent of the norm" (70). Although King occasionally favors an individual authorial voice as the agent of the omniscient perspective, that narrator in The Stand is more conventional: it is generally transparent and rarely the only voice and focus of a narrative unit. When it does modulate into the subjective, it is when the narrative focus is becoming that of an archetypal character. Yet the narrator does demonstrate that it has subjective affiliations (is among the "normal" characters) by a simple but effective device: it regularly refers to members of the protagonist community by their first names, to Flagg by his last. That it even refers to archetypal members of Flagg's Las Vegas community by first name suggests that King wishes to place the antagonist in a special position within the novel.

Danse Macabre also clarifies that special position. King believes that the readers of horror fiction have conflicting needs, a conflict that he addresses by weighing against the normality of the narrator the abnormality of the antagonist, who: offers us a chance to exercise . . . emotions which society demands we keep closely in . . . to indulge in deviant, anti-social behavior by proxy—to commit gratuitous acts of violence, indulge our puerile dreams of power (31). At the end of this essay, I will return to the submerged dynamic processing narrator and antagonist by giving them a locus in the psyche as archetypal character. But for now I want to analyze the technical aspects of perspective. In summary, King's basic point of view in The Stand is omniscient (with very rare authorial presence), serially restricted to the points of view of multiple characters for extended passages, normally a sub-unit within a chapter, occasionally for the full chapter; I will use Bakhtin's term for such passages: zones. In The Stand, a character has clear control of a zone either as focus or voice; only occasionally and generally in a dyadic relationship, e.g. Stu and Fran, does King exercise in this novel the omniscient narrator's option of entering two or more characters' minds during a shared activity. Though ruled by a point of view, the zones are not necessarily ruled by a voice. King often creates a zone in which the character rules by focus (the cinematic eye and ear) rather than voice, one with only inflections of inferiority. In these, should voice make its appearance (which is often), it is as dialogue, henceforth dramatic voice. Such voice is heard rather than shared psychologically; it is other, an objectified experience. Normally, however, dramatic voice is heard by a character (the focus) and is not directly presented to us as would be the dialogue of a play. A good example of the purest dramatic voice in the novel would be Fran's minutes of various Free Zone meetings, recorded for us often as a script; still, it is Fran who is recording and even her most objectified minutes are one sub-form among the documents (the other being her diary) that deliver us her character. The minutes are not objective—they are Fran being objective.

But, just as often, an interior voice may command a zone and our experience of it, particularly when King wants to present the individual psyche rather than relationships. Obviously, narrative crisis peaks—moments of horror, terror, revulsion, madness, rage, savagery, are prime occasions for the voice in horror fiction, for they allow us maximum opportunity to project into the experience of the situation as victim or antagonist. But we also encounter voice frequently outside the crisis peaks: King uses it to create the interior lives of grotesque or unusual figures such as Tom and the Trashcan Man, to create character by allowing us to undergo with it decision and development (especially Larry and, to some extent, Fran), to comply with certain local limitations (Nick's muteness, Harold's conspiracy).

But King has made key tactical decisions to centralize certain characters by extending the zones of interior voice and focus. The characters dominating an extended zone are those which are familiar enough that we may regard them as archetypal personae: distinct, integrated presences commonly found in the communal psyche of a culture such as shadow and mask, anima and animus. Technically, however, all characters (voiced, dramatic, or simply observed) are personae, even those which seem quite unique, not culturally grounded, even the flora, fauna, and terrain of the topography, even events are embodied psychological phenomena, some enduring, some evanescent; and exploring these often silent and ephemeral presences gives us a better grasp of the unexpressed ecology of the novel. But, for this article, I repeat, I will limit myself to some basic groundwork: establishing the dynamics of the voiced, archetypal personae commanding extensive or intense zones.

First, I will present some facts about The Stand's interior voices. Excluding a brief prologue and epilogue, The Stand consists of three books: "Captain Trips" (34% of the novel), "On the Border" (46%), and "The Stand" (20%). The prologue's zone is commanded by the interior voice of one of the plague's first victims, Sally Campion, while the epilogue's is commanded by the antagonist, Flagg. We experience the opening and close of the novel at psychological poles: as victim and antagonist. Within the frame prologue and epilogue provide, the three books have a purposeful circularity of voice: they begin and end with the voice of Stu, one of the few survivors of the novel's protagonistic group and thus the figure closest to being the novel's protagonist, as he first experiences the plague and, six months later, measures its effects upon him and his world.

The zones in Book One are normally chapter-length although the chapters are comparatively short. Book One is most emphatically heteroglossic: commanding significant zones (88% of the book) in this opening third of the novel are those voices which are to become the archetypal personae (Stu, Fran, Larry, Nick, Lloyd, Flagg, the Trashcan Man); Larry commands the broadest zone (22%) with Fran (18%), Stu (16%), and Nick (15%) about equal while the antagonists altogether command only 17% of the book, Lloyd the largest proportion (11%), the Trashcan Man 4%, and Flagg 2%. There is an equal number of minor characters, mostly victims like Sally Campion, commanding a much smaller accumulated zone (12%): the Bruetts, Hapscomb and Palfrey of Arnette; Starkey and Creighton at Blue Base One; Dr. Deitz and Nurse Green at the federal hospital; Lloyd's lawyer and an anonymous photographer; Flagg's first victim, Christopher Bradenton; and four extended authorial zones (Chapters 8, 26, 30, and 38) which provide us the national perspective with occasional appearances of minor characters' interior voices. The zones commanded by minor characters are generally crisis peaks or immediately moving toward such while simultaneously providing us exposition on the enveloping action. The authorial presence extends this dynamic by giving us objectified views, brief anecdotal "clips" of the disaster across the nation.

Book Two's zones typically command narrative sub-units within chapters and the archetypal personae now almost entirely command these zones; chapters are more extensive and heteroglossic although sometimes, particularly when dyads appear in the same zone, voices overlap. While a few new archetypal personae emerge (Abagail, Nadine, and Harold) and a few minor voices (the dog Kojak, Lucy, Judge), the archetypal personae of Book One continue to command this and the last book. Particularly prominent among these (perhaps because she is the secretary for the Free Zone) is Fran, who commands over a quarter of the novel's zones. Abagail, Nadine, and Harold introduce a new agendum into the novel: the fantastic. Abagail, of course, represents God's material wishes while Harold and Nadine remain dramatic voices until Flagg begins to seduce them, whereupon they evolve into interior voices and move from the personal to the archetypal.

With the change of setting to Las Vegas and the introduction of two new plot lines—the Free Zone spies and the Free Zone martyrs, Book Three introduces new voices. The only new archetypal persona of Book Three is Tom although Glen Bateman's (a major dramatic voice throughout) interior voice appears briefly for the first time, just before his death. A minor Free Zone voice is that of the spy, Dayna. Las Vegas appears largely through Lloyd Henreid's consciousness although the Trashcan Man and Flagg have significant presence; there are two minor voices, Angie Hirschfield and Whitney Horgan.

The archetypal interior voices and their inter-dynamics pattern a psyche in process. The interior voices of The Stand, with two exceptions, are in contrasting pairs in reflection of the dualistic process powered by the contest between Abagail and Flagg, the agents of God and Satan. The two exceptions are Bateman and Stu. The one archetypal figure without interior voice (except at his death) Bateman is the thematic voice of the novel, constantly providing us sociological, political, and metaphysical analyses of the situation as it unfolds. Purely conscious, his locus in the novel's psyche is as its superego. Archetypally, he is a familiar figure in the King canon, the Teacher, the understanding Self, the wise man, a major stage on our journey toward the Self, the North Star of the Psyche.

Stu is the novel's traditional protagonist. His position in the novel's psychological locus is at the boundary of super-ego and ego. An undeveloping character, he is, from the beginning, heroic although at first a hero in a world which does not provide opportunity for heroism: a Texan, cowboy, rural, strong, brave, silent, honest, tenacious, but social (the town's sheriff rather than the Lone Ranger). The novel begins with him and ends with him, returning throughout to him during its central processes, always finding a role for him from apocalypse to the founding of the New Jerusalem at Boulder to the mythic encounter of Good and Evil that closes the book. He might have been the protagonist were it not that he never engages the antagonist; King executes that engagement through the contrasted archetypal pairs. So Stu functions as a consistent center, paired with Bateman, Nick, and Fran. With Bateman, he is the consenting audience, the listening hero, who validates and authorizes the thematic character. With Nick, he is executive in the novel's social dynamic. With Fran, he forms a dyad in the novel's romantic dynamic. Mythically, he begins as Ulysses, becomes Remus, and ends as Adam.

The novel's other archetypal personae execute in pairs the its dualistic process: Nick/Lloyd, Larry/Harold, Fran/Nadine, Tom/The Trashcan Man, Abagail/Flagg. Close in psychological locus to Bateman and Stu are Nick and Lloyd, each the central political figure (as opposed to the religious centrality of Abagail and Flagg) of his topography. Through the novel's sociopolitical dynamic, each further exemplifies Stu's process in the novel: the last is to be first. That such is the case demonstrates that the social order destroyed in Book One is corrupt, dying of its own weight, a positive falling away of an organization of society into the impersonal corporation. The corporate dissolved, the archetypal emerges. Each demonstrates that the true leader is informed by and interfaces with the transpersonal, interconnects the political with the cosmic. Each is spiritually clear enough, in his way, to be elected; and for each the clarity comes from disconnection from, and rejection by, the corporate world and a purging of him from it. For each, the election initiates growth. Offered the opportunity to connect politically with society, each shows talent in leadership, negotiation, and organization, especially through his ability to bridge as nexus the purely political and material world of lesser figures and the purely spiritual world of Abagail and Flagg. And each has his limitations: the link to the material blinds each to his fate. Nick doesn't anticipate Harold's bomb (though he typically sacrifices himself to save others) and Lloyd doesn't anticipate the Trashcan Man's (though he stays with Flagg and Las Vegas when others have left). In their fealties lie their fates.

The locus of Larry and Harold in the novel's psyche is the central range: mask and shadow of the ego. For the author, they are closest to a personal presence: with appropriate coloration (blonde and black-haired) and physiques similar to King's (the tall Larry, the tall but fat adolescent Harold), each presents the artist as a figure who can develop the stature to transcend self and to preserve or destroy his world. Unlike the previous characters, this pair develops: unstable from the beginning (Larry corrupted by success, Harold by rejection), each finds his ground and center and fate. The novel repeatedly makes it clear that each man sees his options and makes a choice of his own free will to follow a particular course: Larry chooses to become Christ, Harold Judas.

At a similar level exist Fran and Nadine but they provide the novel its anima, again as mask and shadow. Matched with and completing appropriately their males, Stu and Flagg, each mirrors a different face of the male/female dyad. Nadine mirrors the dyadic relationship as Thanos and joins a Isolde and Juliet in loss and death at the end of obsession. Fran presents love as Eros and joins Eve. For Fran and Nadine function only secondarily in the dyadic relationship. Beyond the romantic and erotic, they are wives and mothers: the future of the species depends upon them. One of the major dramatic questions that powers the novel is: "Will the Child be possible?" It is a question that provides King cliff-hangers to the very end of the novel. The answer is yes. While Flagg and Nadine, the dark Adam and Eve, fail to continue because of the nature of those committed to power and the material, Stu and Fran leave the New Babylon of Boulder to found a New Eden in Maine, where, committed to love, they will care for the new Child.

As is so often the case in a King novel, the Child is key to the human dilemma. In The Stand, however, rather than actual children, we have childlike men, the Trashcan Man and Tom, children of the dark and the light. Rather than beginnings, they are conclusions: Tom is deserted, the Trashcan Man dehumanized, mad. But together they demonstrate the resilience and centrality of the Child. Each functioning as does the Child in terms of his love, Tom preserves the protagonistic Stu while The Trashcan Man destroys the antagonist Flagg. Tom represents the Child as ground for any vital human enterprise: as he joins with Nick, he produces in Nick the charity and eventual love that provide the motive to enact his vision; as he links Nick to Stu, he demonstrates the essential human harmony with the universe, the positive orientation of the natural. Though sided with the Antagonist, The Trashcan Man similarly acts out of his innocent love for Flagg: he brings him what he needs, destruction.

Flagg and Abagail are at the boundary of the psyche approached by Tom: the transpersonal. Abagail's darkness and the spiritual darkness of the "Dark Man" suggest that the locus of these archetypes is in the depths of the psyche. Located beside Satan, God is at the bottom of man, not above. Like Nick and Lloyd, Abagail and Flagg move from the outside in; again, isolation provides clarity. Abagail's biographical flashback illustrating that she represents three enormous, suffering minorities: the female, the black, and the aged. Purified by her suffering, the oldest human being becomes God's choice. In her the mythic archetypes blur: she variously is Job suffering mission without vision, Moses leading the Jews out of Egypt, Christ suffering forty days and forty nights in the desert. In the novel, she introduces the fantastic and the magical that transform it from material disaster to cosmic apocalypse. Beyond Glen Bateman, she is the archetype of the culminating Human: her wisdom surpasses his understanding. She represents our End, our Completion when integration reveals all that was concealed and makes it available to us. If Bateman is the North Star, she is the Galaxy. Her final vision is not cool and ironic: she suffers. If she is what we are to become, it will involve loss and anguish, an understanding of human insignificance, a submission to cosmic process, progress without goal, extinction without reward.

Although the novel establishes him as Abagail's opponent, Flagg is not a perfect contrast to her. Whereas her biography is detailed and dramatized, his is obscure. When we first meet him, Flagg is pretty well on the way to demonic possession: at the end of his first appearance, he levitates; in his second appearance, he psycho-kinetically kills. His memories of identity are dim. We know enough of him to equate him with a figure like Manson, a person who has abused the political and cultural movements of the New Left to indulge a personal drive toward chaos. But even this information suggests that he is more supernatural than personal. The first of the novel's characters to shed identity for archetypal essence, even while he is a person the dimness of his memory, his sense of awakening, and his chameleon nature as an underground agent place him more as an informing spirit of depravity corrupting the cultural movements of the sixties.

If not Satan, Flagg is generally a perfectly competent representative, quite explicitly a demon emissary in possession of a human. His voice is that which King customarily assigns to evil figures: at its peak, it is strong and vivid, graphic, manic, rich in black humor. Externally, though it is capable of such a manic voice when committing savage acts, it develops composure and charisma when manipulating such as Lloyd Henreid. It becomes the voice of a dark deity.

But Flagg is not simply a demon. He develops. Beginning in disorientation, so he ends. When he returns in the third book, his power is much enhanced but his stature much reduced. Processes which he doesn't understand are taking place about him in Las Vegas: his vision and power are limited as his context begins to include those who have not consigned their free will to him: the Judge, Dayna, Tom, Larry, Brentnor, Stu, Glen Bateman. That Bateman names him as "the last magician of rational thought" (742) suggests a nearer locus to the conscious, if not in vision, certainly in tactics. He exists in the world through desire for power and a search for the material tools to obtain it. His is the last effort to control man with technology. And finally this strategy is ineffective, its goal meaningless. King has kept Flagg off the scene for much of the time to characterize him through his impact on others rather than through his personal characteristics. Thus, not only his diminishing when he finally appears in Book Three but the force his absence finally gives to Bateman's last, ironic vision of Flagg: "You are nothing?" and to his last appearance in Book Three as an empty suit of clothes.

Yet the epilogue gives still further status to Flagg. Magically transported to a jungle, he begins again. Our final vision of him is as demon. He may be nothing; but as nothing, he has force. In his emptiness, he gives teeth to the possibility that the universe we inhabit has not only no place for us but no place for anything, is aimless, is absurd, is nothing, an empty suit of clothes.

We now arrive at God. God is veiled. The one voice that we don't hear is His—unless it is the transparent voice of the omniscient narrator set against the vivid and particular voice of the antagonist as uttered by Satan's emissary, Flagg. God also has presence in the continual allusion of the plot to Biblical events: the apocalypse (Captain Trips), the Antichrist (Flagg), Job caught in the contest between God and Satan (Abagail, human suffering), Moses and the migration (Nick and his gathering of people), Christ's forty days and forty nights in the wilderness (Abagail in the desert), the crucifixion (Larry and his two comrades), the creation of Adam and Eve (Stu and Fran leaving for Maine) Besides these shattered glimpses of a cyclical history, a deliberate process re-assembling, is the process by which the bad guys lose and the good guys win, the long, complex, elaborate process that brings together Larry, Flagg and the Trashcan Man at just the moment to destroy the New Babylon, a precise timing that would have been upset by the smallest deviation from the Celestial Script. Nor is this event offered as a random coincidence in a chaotic world. It is a miracle. It is evidence of God.

But is God manifest only in plot? Could He be present in the characterless voice of the narrator, the voice without voice? If so, is this novel finally monologic? Is it "saying" what the speechless God wants it to say? The issue of fate and free will certainly is central to the novel. King's Colorado characters make much of free will: they live in a democracy and debate their decisions; Abagail doesn't command them but presents them their options while they argue with and among themselves about the course they should take; even Harold makes it clear that he choose his course "of my own free will" (978); even given a God, such central characters as Fran and Stu feel free to damn Him for his destructiveness. The issue is the perpetual Christian dilemma: if God is an omniscient and omnipotent creator, am I absolved of my sins? Couldn't He have led me to avoid them? Even forced me? And if not, is not the guilt His? If God is guilty, is he the source of evil as well as of good? King may, then, be re-dramatizing the ancient paradox, one that is most acute with Job.

Or is God simply the author watching his characters work out their own harmonies and dissonances, finding their natural ends, watching his personae do as they must? Is God the Author in the guise of Omniscient Narrator, omniscient but abnegating omnipotence: a perspective either beyond or beneath the personae and thus incapable of action, only capable of being, of recording? Are the personae reassembling the Author? Does He have free will? Or is He subject to the same pulls between being the Shaper and the Shaped? Is His enemy truly Nothing, the possibility that all he, we, have experienced is only fiction? Therein lies the potential horror of The Stand, the "fear in a handful of dust."

This horror is energized by the conclusion of The Stand. The last voice is not God's, if indeed God exists as the normality of the omniscient narrator. It is Flagg's. And he begins again. The novel, finally, then is not monologic. The debate between Satan and God, antagonist and omniscient narrator, persists in its transpersonal depths as it has among the fronted archetypal personae of its cast. To try to resolve this unconcluded process is to move from the ground on which King moves to issues produced by, but external to, the novel.

WORKS CITED

Bakhtin, M[ikhail]. M. The Dialogic Imagination: Four Essays. Trans. Caryl Emerson and Michael Holquist. Ed. Michael Holquist. Austin and London: University of Texas Press, 1981.

Hillman, James. Revisioning Psychology. New York: Harper & Row, 1975.

King, Stephen. Danse Macabre. New York: Berkely Publishing Corporation, 1981. The Stand: The Complete and Uncut Edition. New York: Doubleday, 1975.

McCullaugh, Jim. "Horror Video: September is Horror Month." Billboard 23 Sep. 1989: 54.

Wood, Gary. "The Dark Half." Cinefantastique Feb. 1991: 26.

CHAPTER TEN

Beyond Armageddon: Stephen King's The Stand and the Post-Catastrophic World in Speculative Fiction

Steven E. Kagle

Stephen King's The Stand is part of an ancient tradition. The prophesy and resulting fear of a divinely ordained catastrophe is as old as civilization, appearing in the oldest tales. All of the major religions have some apocalyptic material in their sacred writings. Most of these examples follow a common pattern: the source of the destruction is external, and the result for the righteous who survive the destruction is a rainbow or some other promise of a future free from such catastrophes. Both Greek mythology's fable of Deucallion and Pyrrha and the Hebrew Bible's tale of Noah describe the destruction of Earth by flood and the salvation of a few just people. Similar elements can be seen in the Gilgamesh Epic, The Norse Eddas, and the Hindu Veddas.

Modern science fiction also has its accounts of the destruction of most of humanity and the rescue of a chosen few, but in such works both the proximate and initial causes of the disaster are physical. In Balmer and Wylie's When World's Collide (1933), an early example of such a theme in science fiction, the source of the world's destruction, while not a metaphysical power, is still an external one, Earth's collision with a planetary body. However, especially in the early decades of the "atomic age" and the Cold War, many science fiction writers have created works in which the apocalyptic situation has its origin in human action rather than in natural forces.

Modern science fiction has been profoundly influenced by scientific and technological developments, especially those that have given humans the means to destroy our world while offering little promise for a long or secure future for the survivors of such a cataclysm. Given the more than coincidental association between the creation of these works and the growth of a fear of atomic bombs fostered by the Cold

War, it is to be expected that many of these works such as Walter M. Miller's A Canticle Liebowitz (1959), Roger Zelazny's Damnation Alley (1969), and Harlan Ellison's "A Boy and His Dog" (1969) involve a world ravaged by a nuclear war.[1] However, while much of post-catastrophic science fiction takes place after there has been a "Mad and devastating" war with "lots of bombs and rockets, [and] with a result nobody had predicted" (Damnation 87), others such as Christopher's No Blade of Grass (1956), Frank Herbert's The White Plague (1982), and J.G. Ballard's Burning World (1964) involve an ecological catastrophe.[2] To the extent that the Cold War is over we may expect to see science fiction works relying on such sources of destruction as ecological catastrophe increase and those involving nuclear war decrease.

Science fiction works such as those mentioned above are not always devoid of religious concerns. The tendency within such works for superstitious people to explain a nuclear holocaust or other apocalyptic catastrophe as God's punishment for sin is a common, almost as common as the association of science and technology or any higher learning with sin and attacks on those people associated with such "evils." In The Long Tomorrow (1955), a man denounced as one who is guilty of tempting impressionable young men with the "forbidden serpent's fruit" of urban industrialized society is stoned and torn apart by the mob (20-22); in A Canticle for Liebowitz we learn that the period following the nuclear war was an "Age of Simplification" in which mobs lit "angry bonfires" to burn books (18); in Damnation Alley "the survivors visited the remaining universities . . . and killed the remaining . . . professors. "They shot them, they tore them apart, they crucified them" (87). The general, and the intended effect of such plot elements seems to be to convince the reader that such anti-intellectual attitudes by religious groups are not merely wrong, but that they are also dangerous and immoral.

Occasionally these works may even contain a supernatural element such as Leon Trout,[3] Tor the ghost narrator in Vonnegut's Galapagos (1985), or Benjamin, the strange pilgrim in A Canticle For

Liebowitz, who may be the legendary "Wandering Jew." However, the presence of such an element does not significantly affect the main plot of these works and does not advance the belief in a non-material explanations for the working of the universe. Although in Damnation Alley "the heavens . . . throw garbage," that "heaven" is the physical sky, not the abode of the deity, and that "garbage" is a physical phenomena, not a manifestation of divine retribution (157). It is also significant that the supernatural elements in such works are not sufficiently important to alter the generic identity of these works from science fiction to fantasy.

However, subsequent to that early Cold War period which saw the production of most of the post-catastrophic science fiction noted above, a number of very different works appeared, works that in moving toward fantasy began to bridge the gap between the supernaturally caused apocalypse of ancient myth and the physically caused one of modern science fiction. Among the most important of these works, which include such notable novels as Bernard Malamud's God's Grace (1982), and Robert A. Heinlein's Job: A Comedy of Justice (1984), is Stephen King's The Stand (1978, 1990).[4] In assessing the place of The Stand in post-catastrophic speculative fiction, it is less important that the characters who have survived this cataclysm are not facing "the aftermath of a nuclear war with everything laid to waste" (344) than that their real enemy is spiritual and not physical.

The Stand starts out with a premise that could certainly have been developed as science fiction: a secret germ warfare laboratory creates and accidentally lets loose the superflu, a disease which kills over 99% of the population. But soon (over a 100 pages later, but only 1/10th the way through the novel), a character has a prophetic dream that includes of vision of a mystical *Him* with "burning red eyes"[5] (111). Although other characters begin to have the same experience, this vision does not become reality for another ten chapters at which point we meet the owner of those eyes, Randall Flagg, a man whose "time of transfiguration was at hand," a man who can "suddenly do magic" (184).

Early in the novel one of the officials in a government plague center disclaims responsibility for the superflu, "We are trying to cope with it, all of us. But that doesn't make us responsible ... On this one the responsibility spreads in so many directions that it's invisible" (110). The reader may be inclined to disbelieve this excuse because prior to the point in the novel at which the characters cross an invisible boundary that identifies the transition to the world of magical possibilities, we are looking to blame physical causes and physical agents. It seems plausible to imagine, if not a single culprit, an evil governmental agency such as that in King's abortive television series "The Golden Years." At this point in the novel the reader is still prepared to agree with the doctor who says of the superflu, "I doubt if this is God's doing" (150), but in doing so the reader would be wrong.

Despite the initial pretense that the superflu was created in a biological laboratory, it is not a physical entity. If the superflu had been a "real" disease, it would have had a greater affect on those species that were genetically similar and a weaker affect on those that were genetically very different, but the superflu did not behave in this manner, "it had taken some animals while leaving others alone. It had taken the domestic animals and left the wild ones alone ... The plague had taken man and man's best friends. It had taken the dogs but left the wolves because the wolves were wild and the dogs weren't" (495). Such a selection process seems to defy scientific principles.

One survivor provides an Adventist context for the events taking place by declaring, "We're living out the Book of Revelation in our own time ... how can you doubt it? 'And the seven vials were opened ...' Sure sounds like the superflu to me" (903). King explicitly ties this interpretation to Yeats's poem "The Second Coming" by having another character quote: "What rough beast its hour come round at last, slouches toward Bethlehem to be born?" (176). In a discussion between Stu Redman and Glen Bateman, two of the central characters, the latter approaches the idea of a supernatural agent behind the superflu by citing the appearance of new plagues near the ends of centuries "A malaise which has struck all Western peoples as the century—any century—draws to a close . . . the dancing sickness took place during the latter part of the fifteenth century. Bubonic plague—the black death—decimated Europe near the end of the fourteenth. Whooping cough near the end of the seventeenth." And Stu Redman moves this set of coincidences beyond the physical world citing the appearance of Attila the Hun, Jack the Ripper, and Ted Bundy to argue, "It's during the last three decades of any given century *that your religious* maniacs arise with facts and figures showing that Armageddon is finally at hand." Redman suggest that this crisis was worse than those that had preceded it by noting that, "We are not, after all, simply approaching the centenary this time. We are approaching a whole new millennium" (341).

The heroes and heroines in The Stand do not immediately associate the millennium with the disaster that has destroyed their society. Their initial problems are those that they share with their counterparts in works of postcatastrophic science fiction such as such as Damnation Alley, "A Boy and His Dog," and of difficulties in such areas as communication, transit, and food production caused by the breakdown of technological society: dangers from mobs, gangs, and individual criminals caused by the breakdown of law and order. However, characters in The Stand differ from those in most post-catastrophic science fiction in that they eventually come to a recognize that their survival depends not so much on their overcoming these physical problems as it does on their overcoming a supernatural menace.

The characters' acceptance of this situation is a sign that they have crossed the "magical threshold" of the traditional heroic quest; an undertaking which follows distinctly different pattern than does the "societal quest" of science fiction.[6] Even before they are aware of the implications of such an observation, characters in The Stand declare that their experience is "like being on a quest" (472). They realize that are not in "a living disaster movie" (427) in which their task would be to survive a disaster; rather, they have a particular task to achieve.

In the "societal quest" of science fiction the true hero is a society changed or being changed by the destruction of the old order which metamorphoses through a series of events which are predetermined by forces governed by material or historic determinism. Not all post-catastrophic science fiction involves any sort of quest, but the societal quest pattern is common. The main character of The Long Tomorrow starts out on what he believes is his personal quest to find Bartorstown, the secret installation that has preserved the technology of the past so that he may enjoy it; however, by the end of the novel, he has joined the citizens of Bartorstown in a societal quest which he will never live to see completed, a quest that will inevitably reintroduce the benefits of modern society (hopefully without all of its dangers) to the entire nation. Orson Scott Card's The Folk of the Fringe (1989), while composed of individual stories, ultimately resolves itself into a story of the creation of a new American culture on the ruins of the old, a culture that is the creation not of its individual heroes but of America itself. Card's narrator concludes, "this is what America wanted, what it bent our lives to accomplish" (273).

Although the society in The Stand is profoundly changed as the result of a quest and the success of its questing heroes is not really dependent on their own powers, the pattern of that quest is closer to Joseph Campbell's "monomyth" than to a "societal quest." The heroes are called to the quest by an external power, cross into a realm in which they are aided by magic, and overcome fantastic obstacles to save their society (Campbell, 30). Yet, while King's use of this individual heroic quest pattern links The Stand to a long tradition of works in mythology, folklore, and legend, the novel has a particular feature that sets it apart from most of such works and links it with more contemporary works of speculative fiction such as God's Grace and Job: A Comedy of Justice; this feature is its ambiguous depiction of God, a depiction that makes The Stand seem almost tailor made for a deconstructive reading.

As readers we are tempted by the usual definitions of God as the "all good" and Satan (or his agent) as the "anti-good" to read the main action of the novel as a traditional apocalyptic battle between the forces of that all good and those of the "anti-good." Indeed, King tempts us into such a reading by making most the people brought together in Boulder, Colorado by the telepathic centenarian prophetess Mother Abagail (Abby Freemantle), individuals with whom we sympathize. These individuals, though flawed, seek to do those things which we consider moral and to avoid those things which we consider immoral; while their adversaries, those drawn further west by Randall Flagg are dedicated to an opposite code and exhibit behavior which we find abhorrent. The "good forces" gathered under the banner of God at Boulder not only believe as we do that killing is a crime, but also that in such a post-catastrophic society "the single unforgivable sin . . . [is murder] the taking of a single life" (853). The "evil" forces gathered in the west not only kill, but flaunt such killing by letting the bodies of their crucified victims serve as a warning to those opposed to Flagg.

However, just when we think that the characters we favor have occupied the moral high ground, King's novel gives us reason to question that judgment. It repeatedly shows us that if we refuse blindly to accept traditional labels in identifying good and evil, the meaning of the whole novel may merit revision. Flagg may be "The purest evil left in the world" (514); yet, he may not be the real source of that evil. As Mother Abagail explains, "all things serve the lord" and so even "this black man serves Him too" (515). In this context, Flagg's actions may be blamed on God, a God whose actions defy our usual definition of justice, a God who is "apt to repay service with pain while those who do evil ride over the roads in Cadillac cars. Even the joy of serving him is bitter" (521).

If Flagg's actions are, even if indirectly, controlled by God, then God becomes the source of Flagg's evil. Melville's Ahab raises the same question when he asks, "Is it I, God, or who, that lifts this arm? But if the great sun move not of himself; but is an errand-boy in heaven; nor one single star can revolve; but by some invisible power; how then can this one small heart beat; this one small brain think thoughts; unless God does that beating, does that thinking; does that living, and not . . . Who's to doom, when the judge himself is dragged to the bar?" (445). If God determines all that happens, isn't he ultimately guilty of the sins he causes to be committed?

King explains that "The beauty of religious mania is that it has the power to explain everything. Once God (or Satan) is accepted as the first cause of everything that happens in the mortal world, nothing is left to chance or change"(617). Given the rationale of the novel that its events are the result of some God ordained plan, then the plague, the black man, and all the other evil in the novel are the work of God. Since the black man's actions follow God's plan and advance his will, this "anti-good" is ultimately "all-good," and since God is responsible for all of the killing in the novel, God is guilty of the novel's "unforgivable sin" (853). The characters in the novel are not unaware of this obstacle to their faith. One of the characters even goes so far as to declare of the power that has brought them together: "He's no God he's a daemon," a "Killer God" who, was responsible for "Millions—maybe even billions—dead in the plague and may not be done yet" (918).

This questioning of God's goodness and omniscience is common in a number of modern post-apocalyptic novels and helps to identify the place of The Stand in literary history. In God's Grace Malamud has God admit to Calvin Cohen, the sole surviving human, that though man provided the physical means for the actual holocaust, God allowed it, even willed it to happen: "They [humanity] had not lived according to the Covenant. Therefore I let them do away with themselves. They invented the manner; I turned my head. That you went on living, Mr. Cohen, I regret to say, was no more than a marginal error. Such things happen" (6). At the end of the novel, in an inversion of Abraham's attempted sacrifice of Isaac, Cohen is to be sacrificed by his adopted son, a sentient chimpanzee named Buz. However, unlike the biblical model, no ram is substituted, and Cohen dies. There is no expectation that this ape civilization will fare any better than the human one it has replaced. In Heinlein's Job: A Comedy of Justice we again find that God (Yahweh) has little sympathy for the human race; playing with humans and baiting traps to lure them into contests that

196

they cannot win, He is using them as pawns in silly wagers with Satan (430).

King does not directly condemn this God off hand but, examined closely, that God's behavior seems no more just than that of the versions of the deity in God's Grace and Job. Three of the questing heroes, following God's will, are able to overcome obstacles including their own fear and make their "stand" before Flagg. Mother Abagail had given them hope by declaring, God "brought you here only to send you further on a quest. He means for you to try to destroy this Dark Prince" (917). That instead of destroying this evil, the questing heroes are themselves destroyed is not the ultimate injustice they experience; worse is the fact that their sacrifice means nothing in the final outcome. God does what he could have done all along and like a *Deus ex Machina* plot device, employs his own supernatural power to destroy Flagg and his forces. His action seems worse in that in the process He also destroys the two of the three heroes who were still alive to make their "stand" on His behalf. God's action seems worse still when, at the end of the book, we find that Flagg has not been destroyed at all. Indeed, like the winner of some vast video game, God, having won His game, has pressed "reset." On the final pages of The Stand Flagg has come back to life, found new disciples, and is about the begin the process over again.

In another passage that seems to invite a connection with Moby-Dick, Nadine, the would-be inverse Madonna of the novel, opens her eyes after a vision that anticipates her assignation with Flagg and thinks that she is in Hell. But in her vision "Hell was whiteness, the thesis to the dark man's antithesis. She saw white, ivory bleached-out nothingness" (874). Compare this sentiment with the following in Moby-Dick: "But not yet have we solved the incantation of this whiteness, and learned why it appeals with such power to the soul. it is at once the most meaning symbol of spiritual things, nay, the very veil of the Christian's Deity; and yet should be as it is, the intensifying agent in things the most appalling to mankind.

197

Is it that by its indefiniteness it shadows forth the heartless voids and immensities of the universe, and thus stabs us from behind with the thought of annihilation," (169-70).

This concept is more frightening in The Stand than it is in Moby-Dick because in Moby-Dick mankind's survival is not in doubt even if individual human beings are threatened, while in The Stand events have shown that both the individual and the race are vulnerable. The existence of a supreme being, which might be expected to offer relief from the fear of annihilation offers no comfort. In this novel the terror that King is famous for evoking comes not from Randall Flagg, who pales before most of King's evocations of horror. Instead, its source is a God who seems to treat man as a plaything. It is fitting that The Stand ends not with a rainbow, a thing with a beginning and an end—God's promise that he will never again visit such destruction on the world—but rather with the wheel, a symbol that what has happened once will occur again and again—a warning that beyond Armageddon, beyond the "last battle," lay an endless series of Armageddons:

Life was such a wheel that no man could stand upon it for long.
And it always, at the end, came round to the same place again. (1153)

NOTES

1. Other notable works include Leigh Brackett's The Long Tomorrow (1955) and Orson Scott Card's The Folk of the Fringe (1989 but constructed from stories published between 1985 and 1988).

2. Thomas M. Disch included several such stories in his The Ruins of Earth (1971) including stories such a Daphne Du Maurier's "The Birds" (1953) and Geo. Alec Efflinger's "Wednesday, November 15, 1967" (1971).

3. Son of Vonnegut's fictional novelist Kilgore Trout.

4. Although the best text of The Stand is the 1990 edition which restores hundreds of pages taken out of the original text and which includes some revisions, the important concepts in the work should be associated with the period in which it was first published.

5. References to Flagg's eyes are part of a series of unmistakable allusions to Sauron the Dark Lord of Tokien's of Lord of The Rings. Some examples are: "I have a feeling that he's looking for me and sooner or later I will have to go" (347); "And the a frightful red Eye opened in the dark: vulpine, eldritch. The Eye terrified him yet held him. The Eye beckoned him. To the west where the shadows were even now gathering, in their twilight dance of death" (573); and "Its better not to say much about him after dark" (633). Unwilling to risk the possibility that his readers might miss these associations, King has a character look at one of the black stones with a red flaw that the dark man's disciples wear as some personal palantir and has "a sudden horrible feeling that it was an eye with its contact lens of humanity removed, staring at her as the Eye of Sauron had stared at Frodo from the dark vastness of Barad-Dur in Mordor where the shadows lie" (947).

6. For more on the distinctions between the patterns of the "heroic quest" and the "societal quest," I would refer readers to both Campbell's book <u>The Hero With a Thousand Faces</u> and my article "The Societal Quest."

WORKS CITED

Ballard, J. G. Burning World. New York: Berkley, 1964. Reissued as The Drought, London: Cape 1965.

Balmer, Edwin and Philip Gordon Wylie. When Worlds Collide. J. B. Lippincott, 1932.

Brackett, Leigh. The Long Tomorrow. New York: Del Rey-Ballantine, 1955.

Campbell, Joseph. The Hero with a Thousand Faces. Cleveland: World, 1956.

Card, Orson Scott. The Folk of the Fringe. New York: Tor-Tom Dougherty, 1989.

Christopher, John (Christopher Samuel Youd) No Blade of Grass. New York: Simon and Schuster, 1956.

Disch, Thomas M. Ed. The Ruins of Earth. New York: G. P. Putnam's Son's; Toronto: Longman's, 1971.

Ellison, Harlan. "A Boy and His Dog." New Worlds. April 1969.

Heinlein, Robert. Job: A Comedy of Justice. New York: Del Rey-Ballantine, 1984.

Herbert, Frank. The White Plague. New York: G. P. Putnam's Son's, 1982.

Kagle, Steven E. "The Societal Quest." Extrapolation 12, 1971: 79-85.

King, Stephen. The Stand. New York: Doubleday, 1990.

Malamud, Bernard. <u>God's Grace</u>. New York: Avon Books, 1982.

Melville, Herman. <u>Moby-Dick</u>. Ed. Harrison Hayford and Hershel Parker. New York: W. W. Norton, 1967.

Miller, Walter M. Jr. <u>A Canticle for Liebowitz</u>. New York: Bantam-Lipincott, 1959.

Vonnegut, Kurt. <u>Galapagos</u>. New York: Dell, 1985.

Zelazny, Roger. <u>Damnation Alley</u>. New York: G. P. Putnam's Sons, 1969.

INDEX

A
Abraham 98
Adam 10, 105, 119
Age of Anxiety 4
America 82, 84, 87, 97, 148
American Renaissance 79
Andros, Nick 11, 13, 86, 96, 126, 158
apocalypse, Christian 146
apocalyptic 189
archetype 175
assault 114
atomic holocaust 131
audiences 174

B
Bakhtin, James 177
Bakhtin, Mikhail 173, 174, 175
Barlow 100
Bateman, Glen 4, 8, 11, 13, 42, 51, 52, 103, 104, 110, 133, 179
Bible 59, 90, 92, 98, 104, 113, 154, 189
Biblical 128, 147, 166, 185
Blue, Tyson 48
Bosky, Bernadette Lynn 101
Bradstreet, Anne 70
Bush, George 21, 22

C
Callahan, Father Donald 90, 100
Calvinist 77
Campbell, Joseph 194
Campbell, Ramsey 160
Captain Trips 2, 4, 5
Carter, Jimmy 87
Chan, Leon 85
Chesley, Chris 46

Huxley, Aldous   150

I
interior voice   177
irrationalism   143, 153, 155

J
Jackson, Shirley   53
Jesus   128
Job   92, 94, 183, 185
Job: A Comedy of Justice   196
Jonah   8
Jurgens, Dayna   11, 133

K
Kent State   24, 25
King's style   56
King's women   113, 121

L
Landon, Michael   42
Larry and Harold   181
Las Vegas   16, 30, 115
Lauder, Harold
      13, 15, 22, 30, 73, 75, 76, 80, 86, 100, 117, 137, 138
Lawry, Julie   12
Leverenz, David   85
London, Jack   144
Ludlum   55

M
Magistrale, Tony   4, 8, 11, 85, 90, 92, 101, 134, 135, 145, 147, 150
Maine   46
Manson   183
Marsh, Dave   64
Mason, Bobie Ann   38
Mear, Ben   90, 100
Melville   69, 79, 80, 81, 85, 113, 195